Praise for *Rite of Passage*

If I could live my life as a parent again, I would read this book first. I am folding its words into my works as of right now. Grab several copies of *Rite of Passage*. This is a great gift for a family you love.

> —ANDY ANDREWS, *New York Times* bestselling author of *The Traveler's Gift* and *The Noticer*

Time-tested and proven true in the lives of his own children, Jim McBride's book helps adolescents and parents understand the "rite of passage" into adulthood. With biblical principles, practical advice, and ceremonial guidelines, parents can confidently guide their children into their future as adults. Read this book, follow its principles, and pass a legacy of blessing on to your kids.

> —DR. GARY SMALLEY
> Author of *Guarding Your Child's Heart*

If taken to heart and put into practice, the principles and ideas in this book can help adolescents successfully transition into the kind of Christian adults that glorify the Lord and make parents, grandparents, and pastors happy. They will also help moms and dads become better Christian parents. I recommend it heartily. Every church ought to adopt and support this kind of ministry.

> —WARREN W. WIERSBE, author, a former pastor of Moody Church

Jim McBride is a perfect tag-team partner for any parent. I have grown weary of a lot of the psychobabble that passes for battle-tested advice. Personally, I want to know that the author is a leader at home and at work, I want to know that he's a success at home and at work, and I want to know the spiritual and emotional character of the author's children. I have known Jim McBride for twenty years, I've traveled with him and his family around the world, and I know his children quite well. This mountain of a man stands the tallest when he's on his knees playing with and praying for his children. This book is a must for every parent and grandparent. No more smack down, just time-tested biblical inspiration.

—Dr. Jay Strack
President and Founder
www.studentleadership.net

In a culture where many fathers are abandoning their responsibilities, our children desperately need to understand the significance of their passage into adulthood. Jim McBride's book presents parents with a unique opportunity to intentionally call out their sons and daughters to mature manhood and womanhood. The ceremony that he created is a labor of love and had a powerful impact on his own children. *Rite of Passage* is based on solid biblical principles, and I know Jim's walk matches his talk; therefore I believe there is a blessing in store for those who read this book and follow his example.

—Frank Harrison, Chairman and CEO,
Coca-Cola Consolidated—Charlotte, NC

RITE
OF
PASSAGE
A FATHER'S BLESSING

JIM McBRIDE

MOODY PUBLISHERS

CHICAGO

© 2011 by
JIM MCBRIDE

All Scripture quotations, unless otherwise indicated, are taken from the *New American Standard Bible*®, Copyright © 1960, 1962, 1963, 1968, 1971, 1972, 1973, 1975, 1977, 1995 by The Lockman Foundation. Used by permission. (www.Lockman.org)

Scripture quotations marked ESV are taken from *The Holy Bible, English Standard Version*. Copyright © 2000, 2001 by Crossway Bibles, a division of Good News Publishers. Used by permission. All rights reserved.

Scripture quotations marked NIV are taken from *the Holy Bible, New International Version*®, NIV®. Copyright © 1973, 1978, 1984 by Biblica, Inc.™ Used by permission of Zondervan. All rights reserved worldwide.

Edited by Jim Vincent   Interior design: Ragont Design
Cover design: Rule29
Cover images: Wooden Board on back cover: istockphoto #8047432
    Wood Texture (Seamless) © Wei Ti Ng
    Wooden Path and Field Front Cover: istockphoto #8490828 Wooden
    Walking Path Through Field - Sylt (Germany) © Tobias Helbig
    Sky/Sea Photo Front Cover: istockphoto#10431125
    Dark stormy Sea Waters © Manuel Gutjahr
    Arch Stone Bridge on Front Cover: istockphoto #12339214, Natural
    Stone Arch Charco Manso, El Hierro, Canary Islands © Flavio Vallenari
    Additional Rock/Stone Bridge on Front Cover: istockphoto #13724307
    Owachomo bridge © Aliaksandr Nikitsin
    Front Cover photo illustration by Todd McQueen

Library of Congress Cataloging-in-Publication Data

McBride, Jim.
    Rite of passage : a father's blessing / Jim McBride.
      p. cm.
    Includes bibliographical references.
    ISBN 978-0-8024-5880-3
    1. Father and child—Religious aspects—Christianity. 2. Parent and teenager—Religious aspects—Christianity. 3. Initiation rites—Religious aspects—Christianity. 4. Blessing and cursing. I. Title.
    BV4529.17.M32 2011
    248.8'421—dc22
                                                  2011010273

Also available as an EBook 978-1-57567-876-4

We hope you enjoy this book from Moody Publishers. Our goal is to provide high-quality, thought-provoking books and products that connect truth to your real needs and challenges. For more information on other books and products written and produced from a biblical perspective, go to www.moodypublishers.com or write to:

Moody Publishers
820 N. LaSalle Boulevard
Chicago, IL 60610

1 3 5 9 10 8 6 4 2

Printed in the United States of America

To my children:
Victoria, Buddy, Tommy, and Sarah.

Now the baton passes to you.
May you live out all that your rites of passage
signified, taught, and spoke into your lives.
Because of you, may many more in next generations
know the power of their fathers' blessings
and the powerful love of their heavenly Father.

CONTENTS

Foreword   9
Introduction: Why a "Rite"?   13

1. Rites and Blessings   25
2. Developing the Idea   39
3. Buddy's Rite of Passage   57
4. Tommy's Turn   71
5. Victoria's Rite   83
6. Sarah's Turn   97
7. Planning a Rite of Passage   107
8. Outcomes   127

Epilogue: It's Never Too Late   133
Appendix: Sample Outlines for Planning
          a Rite of Passage   141
Notes   145
Acknowledgments   147

FOREWORD

I know Jim McBride on multiple levels. I first got to know him as his pastor. Jim and his family were new in town and visited Sherwood. He was the new manager for the Coca-Cola plant in Albany, and it didn't take long for me to discover that this man was a leader.

I've known him as a Sunday school teacher, faithful deacon, chairman of our school committee, and now as a staff member. In every capacity, Jim has modeled integrity, a commitment to excellence, and a passion for things eternal.

Ten years ago, Jim came on our staff and serves as my executive pastor. He runs the day-to-day operations for a multimillion dollar church budget and has guided us through four significant capital campaigns geared to reaching the next generation for Christ. He's given guidance to the completion of Legacy Park, our 82-acre sports complex built with the sacrificial gifts of our membership and monies from Sherwood Pictures.

In addition, he oversees all the contracts and financial arrangements for Sherwood Pictures. I think you can see that Jim's a busy man. We have traveled across the country these last few years to churches, conferences, big events, and media interviews to talk about what God was doing through the movies *Flywheel, Facing the Giants, Fireproof,* and *Courageous.* When you spend as much time together as we do, you begin to know each other on multiple levels.

Jim is not only a co-laborer and my executive pastor, he is my friend. He knows me inside and out and still chooses to love me and stand with me as we seek to reach the world from Albany, Georgia. I couldn't imagine being on this journey without him.

But this book is not about how many plates he spins for Sherwood Church. It's about Jim as a husband and father. Even with all his responsibilities, Jim has proven himself to be a godly man with an unwavering commitment to his wife and kids. I honestly don't know how he finds the time to do all he does, but he does it.

Jim has four grown children. When I first met this family, his kids were much younger. Now three of them are married, and there are grandkids in the picture. Jim's children love and honor their dad. I've watched and listened as his children have sought him for wisdom and direction. He is a good and godly guide to them. He offers them nuggets of truth on which they can build their lives. This book is not Jim's "idea"—it's his life. It's how he has lived out being a godly man, husband, and father.

The book you hold in your hands is special. It was born, not out of theory, but out of practice. Each of Jim's children has walked through this rite of passage. You will get to know Jim in this book, and you'll love his heart. You'll see the commitment he and Sheila have to developing their kids into

Christ-followers. They have all received their father's blessing, and they know both the strong personality and tender heart of their dad. These young men and women are evidence of a man who has guided his household in truth.

In a day when so many homes are lacking a father who leads, this book is a much-needed resource. It will encourage you, wherever you are with your children or grandchildren, to set the bar high. I encourage you to read this book and then make personal application of the truths and examples in your own family.

> Michael Catt
> Senior Pastor, Sherwood Baptist Church
> Executive Producer, Sherwood Pictures

WHY A "RITE"?

Why does anyone need a book on a rite of passage?

Because inviting a teenager into adulthood on purpose is better than letting it happen by accident. I believe it is part of our God-given responsibility in the stewardship of the lives of our children to call out the man in our boys and the woman in our girls. Let me explain.

I grew up in a traveling carnival family. Our family traveled the East Coast, everywhere from Bridgeport, Connecticut, to Florida; twice we even put our equipment on a barge and went to Venezuela and Puerto Rico. As a "carny," I had my first job at seven, working in the carnival during the summer.

When I was nine, my great-uncle Woody bought me an ice cream stand. It was my own business, and I got to hire, fire, and manage people, and buy all my stock—basically I ran the whole thing. I remember once that year getting ready to play the West Virginia State Fair. The day before we opened for business, the milkman came by to see if the ice cream stand needed any ice cream stocked. I told him I did need some supplies, to which he replied, "Hey kid, I need to talk to the owner."

I told him I was the owner; his response to this was to get in his truck and drive on down to my uncle's larger concession stand.

When he asked my uncle if he needed anything for his ice cream stand, my uncle told him that the man who owned the ice cream stand was at the ice cream stand. The milkman said the only person up there was a little kid. My uncle told him, "That little kid owns it, and if you want to sell stock, that is the man you have to deal with." Pretty soon he was back to see me for the order.

The Carny Life

Through this kind of on-the-job-experience, my uncle gave me an early education about many lifelong experiences. I graduated from there to managing one of the big rides, the Tilt-A-Whirl, when I was fifteen. I was responsible for tearing it all down, putting it back up, and hiring the crew to do it.

I started driving when I was about twelve, tooling down the interstate with my uncle in the passenger seat. By the time I was sixteen, I was driving bigger trucks. I continued that process of increased responsibility in the carnival world until I was eighteen years old. Needless to say, our lifestyle was not very conducive to being in church every Sunday. I went only when we were home, and then I just went through the motions and said the right words. This "faith" had not touched my heart or affected the way I lived.

At eighteen, I joined the US Marine Corps. I went to boot camp—itself a rite of passage—and then went on to become a communications specialist, working with radios and other communications gear. But I was still a carny and a businessman at heart. The many skills I'd picked up in that trade would serve me well in the civilian world. So after my stint in the Marines, I used my natural inclination for business and jumped right in. I joined the Coca-Cola Company in 1985 as a deliveryman and later became a route salesman. I quickly rose to management ranks, beginning as an assistant supervisor in a Greensboro, North Carolina, distribution plant.

Six years earlier, after I had returned home from Marine Corps boot camp, I had begun to date my Sheila, the girl I would one day marry. I knew by our second date that this was the woman I would spend the rest of my life with. She was a Christian, and eventually she would love and pray me into the faith. Over the next ten years we would have our four children who have been the greatest blessings of our lives.

Learning about Wrestling, Coca-Cola, and Being a Man

In the meantime, I'd developed an additional skill-set. Football had been a big part of my life growing up, and I'm a pretty big guy, so, naturally, I thought I would try my hand at professional wrestling. As a side "business" in North Carolina, I became one-half of the professional wrestling tag team Destruction, Inc.

At that point I had been affiliated with Coke for two years, so my ring name was Sergeant Sprite. I introduced myself to my fans this way: "I'm 245 pounds of twisted steel and sex appeal! The man with the power, too sweet to be sour! Women wanna love me, men wanna fight me! I'm the king of sting, the freight train of pain! Wooooh, baby! Ain't I pretty?"

Okay, so I wasn't exactly humble. My partner and I lasted eighteen months and won lots of fans, but I quit after one of our opposing wrestlers put a dangerous move on me that he agreed he wouldn't use—he could have broken my neck!

I was driven to succeed in business and rose quickly up the Coca-Cola corporate ladder. That led to my being in Burlington, North Carolina, in the early 1990s, managing a Coke plant with about a hundred employees. I attribute my position to hard work but also to the principles I learned in the carnival trade from my great-uncle, Woody McBride. My business training proved invaluable since I learned how to manage people from a very early age.

But I didn't get a lot of training on what it really meant to be a man.

At this point—I was thirty-two—I had not attended church in eight years, other than for a wedding or a funeral. Through a series of circumstances, no doubt engineered by God, I overheard some coworkers talking about their faith. The Lord was tugging at my heart, and when I heard one of the men inviting another to visit his church, I actually butted in and asked why he didn't invite me. Of course, he immediately did.

I went home and told Sheila that I had accepted an invitation to church, and her reaction . . . well, let's just say she was astonished. As a believer, she had been praying for me. For eight years she had even been bringing her Christian friends to the house in the hope that something would rub off and I would give my life to Christ.

The Leader Who Wasn't Leading

We went to church the next Sunday morning, which happened to be Super Bowl Sunday, and the pastor's message was, "Whose Team Are You Quarterbacking: God's or Satan's?" He asked, "Are you leading people to heaven or hell with your actions?" It was as though he was speaking directly to me. I wasn't an idiot—I knew I was a leader, and I sure wasn't leading anyone to heaven. I wasn't focused on the Lord; I was focused on myself. People looked up to me because I was successful, but my model of "success" was different from the Lord's, and I was leading people astray with my actions.

The pastor said, "It doesn't matter whether you're the sweeper or the CEO at a company—there is somebody who looks up to you. There is somebody you have influence over, somebody who is modeling their life after yours." I felt convicted for the first time. Could it be true that my actions were leading people to hell?

I went back to work that week and couldn't think of much else except what God had said to me through that pastor's faithful preaching. One day, I called five guys I knew to be Christians into my office. I asked them questions, and they shared their faith. After some time, I said to them, "I know for certain what I need right now is Jesus Christ as my Lord and Savior. Can you help me? Show me what to do?"

One of the guys said, "I have to go to my car and get my Bible." When he brought the Bible in, I remember thinking that it had to be his wife's, because it had this lacy covering. Looking back on it now, this is humorous, but it just goes to show that when God is moving, little things like that don't matter.

He opened the Bible and shared Scripture with me, and then I knelt in my office with those five men and prayed to receive Christ.

Once I had accepted Jesus as my Savior, God gave me a tremendous passion for making sure that Sheila and I, as a couple, passed on the torch of the gospel of Christ to the four wonderful children God blessed us with: Victoria, Buddy, Tommy, and Sarah. We wanted to give them a better foundation and guidance to prepare them for their life's journey.

The road that led me to understanding the importance of

being specific and intentional in leading my children toward adulthood (as young men and women, and also as followers of Christ) seemed long. But now, I was ready for the awesome responsibility and pleasure of stewarding these young lives into manhood and womanhood.

Why a Rite?

Though the relationship I had with my father was good, I never knew if he truly believed in me and if I had his blessing. I had no experience of him blessing me and sending me into the world as a man. I wanted it to be different for my own sons.

I love to read, and not much later I learned about a rite of passage from several books, including Robert Lewis's *Raising a Modern-Day Knight: A Father's Role in Guiding His Son to Authentic Manhood*. Using the process by which a boy moved through the various stages of knighthood during medieval times as an example, Lewis identified similar stages for use by today's fathers. From these he created ceremonies in which fathers could commemorate significant milestones in a young man's journey toward becoming a man. Lewis writes:

> In my estimation fathers today are coming up short with their sons at three critical points. First, we have failed to deliver to our sons a clear, inspiring, biblically grounded *definition of manhood*. . . . Telling a boy to "be a man" without defining manhood is like saying, "Be a success." It sounds good. But practically, it takes you nowhere.
>
> Second, most fathers lack a *directional process* that calls their sons to embrace the manhood they should be able to define. Typically, what passes for masculine training in most homes is vague and hit-or-miss. . . . [I]t handicaps a son in knowing how to move out of childhood and into

manhood. What he needs is a specific language and training that takes him to the place where, like the apostle
Paul, he can say, "When I became a man, I did away with
childish things."

A third shortcoming involves the loss of *ceremony*.[1]

These few paragraphs moved me, and I was determined not
to let that happen to my boys. I had slid into manhood without a definite ceremony or a knowledge of what being a man
is about. I had needed then something of ceremony and sub-
stance, and so did my boys now. After praying about it, I told
Sheila, at the appropriate time, I wanted to do some kind of
rite of passage for Buddy and Tommy, something that was
unique to them as boys and to our family. It would be something that would help them understand what it means to be
a man.

I would create a deliberate process to move them toward
that goal. And, as Lewis wrote, I wanted to commemorate the
process with a specific ceremony to mark their entrance into
manhood—an event that would cap the entire process. First,
I wanted to set a specific date and time when I would recognize my son as a man in his father's eyes. Second, I wanted to
gather a group of godly men. These men would be from among
those who already invested in my son's life. They would be
people who my son could call on for godly support—a godly
counsel group or a spiritual accountability group.

Later, I would adapt this model for my daughters, Victoria
and Sarah.

I encourage you to do something similar. This book contains
the process that I have used to take our four children through
their rites of passage, but please note that it is not intended to
be a one-size-fits-all guide. Each family is different, and each
child is different. I hope that through the following pages you

will pick up general principles and adapt them to your particular circumstances.

Preparing Our Children Right

I can't stress enough the importance of doing this. Our culture is growing increasingly hostile to living out Christianity, and we cannot just send our children into the world unprepared. If we do, chances are they'll drift away from the faith.

A recent study by LifeWay Research[2] found that seven in ten churchgoing people ages eighteen to thirty—both those who went to an evangelical church and those who went to a more mainline church—had quit attending services by age twenty-three. And 34 percent of those said they had not returned, even sporadically, by age thirty. This means that about one in four young people have left the church. This is similar to research conducted by the Barna Group, which found that a majority of today's twentysomethings had been churched at one point during their teen years but were now spiritually disengaged, i.e., not actively attending church, reading the Bible, or praying. Only one-fifth of twentysomethings have maintained a level of spiritual activity consistent with their high-school experiences.

David Kinnaman, president of the Barna Group, wrote:

It's not entirely surprising that deep, lasting spiritual transformation rarely happens among teenagers; it's hard work at any age, let alone with the distractions of youth. And since teenagers' faith often mirrors the intensity of their parents', youth workers face steep challenges because they are trying to impart something of spiritual significance that teenagers generally do not receive from home.[3]

As a pastor and as a parent, I find these statistics depressing, and that last statement should be a three-alarm warning for all Christians. While student workers and ministers in our churches do great work—you'll hear about a few of them in this book—it is *not* their job to raise your children in the way they should go. They are there to reinforce what we as parents should already be doing. As the Barna study says, our teens' faith mirrors the intensity of their parents' faith. If they're not getting it at home, it's doubtful the student pastor at church, having at most a few hours a week with your child, will be able to have much influence by himself.

Ed Stetzer, director of LifeWay Research, said, "Too many youth groups are holding tanks with pizza. There's no life transformation taking place. People are looking for a faith that can change them and to be a part of changing the world."[4]

There is good news, though. The LifeWay survey found that those who stayed with or returned to church as young adults had more than likely grown up with parents who were committed to the church and with church members who had invested in their spiritual development.

That's where you come in. The Christian rite of passage is a unique way to confer on your children a blessing and a confirmation of their role in the faith. It's a way of telling them that they are special and that you, the parent, the grandparent, the guardian, the friend, take a special interest in their lives, even as they move beyond the home into their adult lives. Brian Molitor talks about this in his book *Boy's Passage, Man's Journey*:

> Parents do their level best to equip their sons with all they need to succeed. Nutrition, tuition, transportation, lectures, and love—all have been liberally supplied. Surely this is sufficient for our young men to prosper.

Or is it?

If these basics are all a young male needs to succeed, then why are so many in our society struggling to find purpose, identity, and manhood itself? Why are so many men, young and old, depressed or anxious about life? What could possibly cause today's endless stream of horror stories involving crime, teen sex, drug and alcohol abuse, gangs, murder, and suicide?[5]

The problem is that so many men today never learned what it *really* means to be a man. Who are their role models? They're surrounded by a culture of casual drug and alcohol use. Hollywood and pop culture tell a man that he is defined by how many women he sleeps with, or how tough he is. Some, craving approval from adults and peers, join gangs. One of the appeals of gangs is that they promote themselves as a family. If you join, you become part of that family. (And don't think gangs are just an inner-city problem. The FBI recently warned that they're increasingly moving into the suburbs and even rural areas, where they're finding fertile ground in aimless and alienated young people.[6]) The despair that comes from such a culture leads our youth into self-abuse such as cutting and eating disorders and, for some, suicide.

Many young adults were never affirmed in the process of growing up. They most likely did not have a group of men or women to guide them and provide the lifelong counsel a young person needs to move from adolescence into adulthood. Our culture cries out for this guidance—we've got to deliver it.

This book contains the process I used to take my four children through their rites of passage, a process customized to our needs but one easily adapted to other families and their particular situations. I'll show you how some other families have personalized the rite of passage, and I'll provide advice on planning a rite of passage for your children.

The challenge is being laid down for Christian dads (and moms) to take purposeful direction in the lives of their children, to mark as significant a time in their children's lives when they became a man or a woman, to have a day when they acknowledge this milestone in the presence of others who have had and will continue to have a lasting and meaningful impact on their lives.

Let's start the journey!

One

RITES
AND BLESSINGS

Many civilizations throughout history have celebrated rites of passage, signifying a coming-of-age milestone. There's something in our nature that makes us want to acknowledge a transition from childhood to adulthood. Typically those rites have included three elements: *separation, transition,* and subsequent *incorporation.*

In the *separation* phase, the young person is taken from his familiar environment to enter a different and sometimes difficult world. Separation can take many forms: a distant journey, a trial in the wilderness, or just a time away from parents.

During the *transition* phase, the initiate must undergo some sort of change, whether it be a trial of arms, a survival challenge, or increasing responsibility. The transition phase is the time where the participant learns the appropriate behavior for the new stage he is entering. Whatever the transition event is, the person is different when he emerges from what he was when he began.

Finally, during *incorporation*, the young man or woman is welcomed back into the larger society, hopefully as a transformed person with a new sense of purpose and mission. This last phase takes place when the young person is formally admitted into the new role, and it often features a ceremony of some sort.

Be a Marine!

In a way, my experience in Marine Corps boot camp was a rite of passage. During *separation* I left my family and everything I knew, and I journeyed to Parris Island, South Carolina, the Marine boot camp of legend. Upon getting off the bus to the shouts of Marine drill instructors, I was ushered through a door that read, "Through These Portals Pass Candidates for the World's Finest Fighting Force." I was truly separated, in a world where we recruits could never do anything fast enough or right enough. (I have to confess that early on I found myself asking, *Mama, what have I done?!*) Parris Island is not separated just in the sense that you are cut off from your past; it is literally separated from the US mainland, joined only by a single causeway, guarded by an armed sentry.

During *transition*, I was slowly molded into a US Marine. It was a long, arduous process, with a lot of long days involving hours in the field, in classrooms, and on the "grinder" (that's what Marines called the large parade deck where close-order drill takes place). But slowly, through the three phases of Marine Corps recruit training, I was changing from a civilian with civilian habits into a Marine with Marine habits.

Finally, months later, came the day for graduation, when I would be fully incorporated into the Marine Corps. On that day I was granted the title "US Marine" for the first time. (During boot camp, we were called only "recruit," "private," or words I can't repeat here, but never "Marine." That title had to be earned). On that day of *incorporation* I joined a fighting force with a rich, two-hundred-year tradition and the esprit de corps and camaraderie that comes with it. I was now a member of something much larger than myself, with an entire tradition of honor, courage, and commitment to uphold. Equally important to me was the moment when I was also reintroduced to the welcoming embrace of my family.

Becoming a Man in Sparta

Other cultures throughout the centuries have incorporated rites of passage that bring their young people—usually boys—into the wider world of that culture. In ancient warrior cultures such as Sparta, Greece, this rite was brutal, and sometimes the young man didn't survive. The separation phase began early, usually when the boy was only about seven. He was trained in the art of war and lived under severe, sparse conditions (hence our word *spartan*, meaning harsh, tough, devoid of luxury). During those years he learned discipline and physical and mental toughness.

Once he reached age eighteen, the young man was given only a knife and sent into the wilderness to survive by his strength and wits. Those who survived until age twenty were finally welcomed into the full ranks of the Spartan military, where they served until age thirty. The Spartan rite of passage prepared a young man for the thing most prized by the culture of Sparta: the warrior's life.

How Maasai Youth Become Men

Such rites of passage still continue today. They feature similar themes, but are more directly tied to contributing to the wider society. Jerry Moritz, a retired US Navy chaplain who spends many summers ministering to the Maasai tribe of Africa, relates their rite of passage.[1] The Maasai are a seminomadic pastoral people whose territory covers southern Kenya and parts of Tanzania. Their entire culture centers on their cattle, their source of food and their measure of wealth. They surround their villages with high barriers of acacia bushes with inch-long thorns that no lion, leopard, hyena, or even elephant can breach. At night they drive their livestock into the compound to protect them from predators. But the cattle must have room to range, so during the day they are herded onto the African veldt. There their main enemy is the lion. For obvious reasons, then, the Maasai rite of passage revolves around a lion hunt.

When young Maasai boys reach the age of fourteen or fifteen, they are taken out into the bush by the *morans*—the warriors of a particular family group. The *morans* form a circle around a male lion, the young man is given a shield and a spear, and he is ushered into the circle with the lion. These initiations are very fluid and fast-moving. It's young boys against a wily predator that is stronger and faster than they. Moreover, the lion feels trapped by the circle of warriors and becomes even more dangerous. The boy must kill the lion before the lion kills him. If there is a group of boys undergoing the initiation, according to tradition, the first boy to throw his spear and wound the lion gets the credit for the kill. If the lion evades efforts and then attacks the boy, the warriors will come to his defense and kill the lion, but the boy has not passed the rite.

If a young man successfully kills the lion, he is considered successful in the rite of passage and becomes a *moran*. But he is not finished. He must separate himself from the larger group for a time. He lives out in the bush for six to eight years and lives off the land. Sometimes he will link up with other new *morans* who have successfully gone through the same rite. They are allowed to kill the occasional goat or a cow for food, even though it may belong to another Maasai group. During this time a new *moran* also looks for a wife. He may go into a Maasai compound, go to any of the huts, and thrust his spear into the ground inside the hut. The woman in the hut, according to tradition, then becomes his wife. Once the new *moran* has completed his time out in the bush, he returns to his village and is considered an elder among the Maasai. The Maasai rite of passage prepares the young man to receive all the skills and courage needed to become a protector of his people.

The Meaning of the Bar Mitzvah

Another rite of passage perhaps more familiar to readers is the Jewish bar mitzvah, which literally means "son of the commandment." The variant for girls is bat mitzvah, with *bat* meaning "daughter." Jewish tradition states that until the age for this rite, children are under their father's authority and not directly responsible to God for keeping His commandments. Upon becoming a bar or bat mitzvah, though, the child is responsible directly to God for keeping the law.

Technically, the term refers to the child who is coming of age—thirteen for boys, twelve for girls—not to the ceremony itself. However, you are just as likely to hear that someone is "having a bar mitzvah" or "invited to a bar mitzvah." No bar mitzvah ceremony is actually needed. A Jewish boy or girl automatically becomes a bar mitzvah or bat mitzvah upon reaching the appropriate age. The bar or bat mitzvah ceremony is not mentioned in the Jewish Talmud and is a relatively modern innovation. The receptions or parties that are commonplace after the bar or bat mitzvah today were unheard of as recently as a century ago.

There is a special religious significance to being bar or bat mitzvah. Under Jewish law, children are not obligated to observe the commandments, although they are encouraged to do so as much as possible to learn the obligations they will have as adults. Once of age, though, children must observe the commandments. The bar mitzvah ceremony formally and publicly marks the assumption of that obligation, along with the corresponding right to take part in leading religious services, to count in a *minyan* (the minimum number of people needed to perform certain religious services), to form binding contracts, to testify before religious courts, and to marry.

In its earliest and most basic form, a bar mitzvah is the celebrant's first *aliyah*, i.e., reading from the Torah in Hebrew or reciting a blessing over the reading during services, which is considered an honor. Today, it is common practice for the bar mitzvah celebrant to do more than just say the blessing. It is most common for the celebrant to learn the entire *haftarah* portion (the reading of the prophets), including its traditional chant. In some congregations, the celebrant reads the entire weekly Torah portion, leads part of the service, or leads the congregation in certain important prayers. The celebrant is also generally required to make a speech, which begins with the phrase, "Today, I am a man." The father traditionally recites a blessing. In modern times, the religious service is followed by a celebration that is often as elaborate as a wedding reception.

For the bat mitzvah, in some Jewish practices the girls perform essentially the same ceremony as the boys. In more conservative wings of Judaism, though, women are not permitted to participate in religious services in these ways, so a bat mitzvah, if celebrated at all, is usually little more than a party. The bar mitzvah or bat mitzvah prepares the young man or woman to be a full member of a Jewish family and congregation, accountable to both his family and to God.

Granting the Blessing

The Blessing in the Old Testament

From Judaism we also get the idea of sending our young people into the world with a blessing from God, a priest, a patriarch, or one's father. The biblical blessing takes many forms, but a key idea in blessing is to set aside someone or something for a special, holy purpose. It can also mean to praise or glorify as well as to keep and protect.

An early blessing is found in Genesis 14:18–19 (NIV), where Melchizedek blesses Abram (soon to become Abraham): "Then Melchizedek king of Salem brought out bread and wine. He was priest of God Most High, and he blessed Abram, saying, 'Blessed be Abram by God Most High, Creator of heaven and earth.'" It was a way of calling down God's favor on Abram and acknowledging God's provision in the past (victory in battle) and in the future (God's covenant with Abraham).

Another blessing is found in Genesis 48, as Jacob lies dying. His entire family is reunited, and he knows his long-lost son, Joseph, has had God's special calling upon him. And because of the promise God had made to Jacob through his grandfather and father, Abraham and Isaac, Jacob is determined to pass this blessing not just to his own sons, but to Joseph's sons born when he was in Egypt: Ephraim and Manasseh.

> [Jacob] blessed Joseph and said, "The God before whom my fathers Abraham and Isaac walked, the God who has been my shepherd all my life to this day, the angel who has delivered me from all evil, bless the lads; and may my name live on in them, and the names of my fathers Abraham and Isaac; and may they grow into a multitude in the midst of the earth." (Genesis 48:15–16)

Not only does the mention of Abraham and Isaac connect Jacob's faith in God to his immediate forefathers, but it also helps tie together the faith of the earliest patriarchs in Genesis —those who were said to have walked with God—with that of Abraham, Isaac, and Jacob. It harkens back to past blessings and becomes a continuation of those blessings to future generations. It is a confirmation and promise of God's faithfulness.

Another blessing for future generations can be found in the so-called blessing of Moses, found in Deuteronomy 33:1–29. Here the patriarch pronounces blessings on the tribes of Israel, reminding them that it was God's provision and love that has blessed them.

The Blessing of Jesus

Perhaps the most important blessing in the Bible is found in the accounts of Jesus' baptism in the first three Gospels (Matthew 3:13–17; Mark 1:9–11; Luke 3:21–22). John the Baptist had been preparing the way for the Messiah, baptizing people with water, but he promised that another, greater than he, would soon come. One day Jesus Himself came to John and said it was proper for Him to be baptized, "to fulfill all righteousness." Upon coming up out of the water, Jesus saw heaven opened and the spirit of God, in the form of a dove descending upon Him. And God's voice from heaven said, "This is my Son, whom I love; with him I am well pleased" (Matthew 3:15, 17 NIV).

This statement directly from God was His blessing on His Son, the promised Messiah. It marked the beginning of Jesus' public ministry, with God clearly communicating to His Son that He was sent forth with His Father's praise and with His blessing.

Interestingly, Jesus' first recorded experience after being sent on His mission with His Father's blessing was His temptation in the wilderness of the desert. That wilderness was associated not only with demonic activity, but it also was the place where Israel faced her greatest testing.

The Benefits of Blessing Your Child

The blessing that concludes a rite of passage gives security and comfort to your children as they get ready for adulthood. You are their advocate. They have your support and all that goes with it. A lot of men lack confidence because they never had the support of their fathers. There's something special about the public acknowledgment of the father for the son.

A blessing on a daughter is equally important. Many girls get off track in life because their relationship with their father was disconnected. And seeing a father as a man leading a life of integrity sets up a daughter to do the same. The father sets an example in her mind of what it means to be a man. . . and hopefully a godly man. It makes a father want to be a lot more guarded in living a life with Christ.

By giving this blessing to his son and daughter, the father sets up the son and daughter for a head start in life, avoiding mistakes that many young adults make. In contrast, a child's maturity often is stunted by the broken relationship with the father.

Giving your children a formal blessing is similar to Israel's blessing on his sons, calling out each child and giving a specific blessing that acknowledges each child's adulthood and conveys your support. There will be other opportunities to express your love, but this day presents a special opportunity to affirm your children. (For specifics on the prayer of blessing, see the end of chapter 2.)

What to Include in
Your Child's Rite of Passage

From Jesus' desert experience we can learn some important things to include, literally or figuratively, in the rites we use for our children. In Jesus' case, His desert sojourn was a literal separation from civilization. The Judean wilderness is a barren land. It is not a sandy desert like you might see in the movies; rather, it is a wasteland of rocks and boulders, steep drop-offs, and yawning caverns: no water, no plant life—nothing. But Jesus was not totally alone. He had fellowship with his Father and the Spirit, and He had the Word of God in His heart.

Separation

So here's lesson one: The *separation* phase must include some spiritual aspect. The separation does not have to be a literal wilderness—any sense of being taken out of the normal day-to-day world should suffice. The key is that the separation focuses on your child's spiritual being. It cannot be wilderness adventure solely for the sake of wilderness adventure.

Here's lesson two: Any rite of passage must be grounded in God's Word, and there should be ample use of it throughout. Jesus would be repeatedly tempted; each time, He referred to God's Word in response.

Transition

Jesus' time in the wilderness was a time of *transition*. He was moving from His life as a young Jewish carpenter toward the ministry His Father had prepared for Him. Jesus knew what His ultimate mission was: to suffer and die for our sins. Being fully God yet fully human, He was able to be tempted, which is what Satan had prepared for Him.

The Devil offered Jesus three temptations to turn away from the Cross. There are various interpretations as to why Satan tested Jesus with these three particular things—turning stones into bread, being saved from certain death from a high fall, and being given all the kingdoms of the world. In some ways these temptations experienced by Christ are similar to those mentioned in 1 John 2:16 (the lust of the flesh, the lust of the eyes, and the pride of life). John Wesley defines them in his commentary:

> The desire of the flesh—the pleasure of the outward senses, whether of the taste, smell, or touch. The desire of the eye—the pleasures of imagination, to which the eye chiefly is subservient; of that internal sense whereby we relish whatever is grand, new, or beautiful. The pride of life—all that pomp in clothes, houses, furniture, equipage, manner of living, which generally procure honor from the bulk of mankind, and so gratify pride and vanity. It therefore directly includes the desire of praise, and, remotely, covetousness. All these desires are not from God, but from the prince of this world.[2]

These are three battlegrounds our children will face as well. We need to prepare them for the right response. Therefore, any rite of passage must be grounded in God's Word.

Finally, wrap up your rite of passage with your own form of feasting, whether it be a family meal at home or a fancy outing in a restaurant. After Satan failed in his attempts to short-circuit Jesus' mission, he left, and angels then ministered to Jesus. This was a way of being reincorporated into the world, and also a time of celebration.

Incorporation

For your son or daughter, this time of celebration and sharing is a final grace note to tell the young man or woman that they are now part of a larger society. It's a way of welcoming them into the fellowship. This is *incorporation*. With your son or daughter seated in a chair, all of the adult participants surround your son or daughter and pray on their behalf. Then you conclude by praying the blessing upon your child as those partners stand as witnesses. The prayer of blessing should take place at the end of the ceremony of passage. It is the climax, the last thing your child will hear as you conclude the rite of passage.

Such a ceremony is neither frivolous nor empty of meaning. When we lead our children into their rite of passage and bestow a blessing, we help deliver them from our age's own form of wilderness. Today we live in a society that has various ideas about what it means to come of age. On a basic level, the world tells young people they've made this transition to adulthood when they leave their mom and dad's home, join the military, or enter college. More ominously, the world tells our young people that they have gone through their rite of passage when they've drunk their first beer, smoked their first cigarette, participated in sexual activity, gotten a tattoo, or used various other ways of rebelling against God and/or their parents.

Too often, there is no rite or no celebration of entering adulthood at all. *Too often, our young people simply drift into adulthood with no sense of commission or blessing from their society or their families.*

I believe as Christian parents we are charged to make clear for our kids when the time comes for their rite of passage. As with other cultures, I think our rite of passage has to be deliberate—something the child knows will happen at a certain time. It should not be a surprise that it will happen, although elements of the ceremony itself can be kept secret until the proper time.

The Celebration

The rite ends with celebration. Celebrate with a meal full of good conversation among the adults. Let your child listen and invite him to participate. Now he is among the adults . . . he is an adult in your eyes and his. You are sending him or her forth with an explicit blessing that ties into the family heritage, God's trustworthiness, and His provision. Enjoy the food and fun. Let your child sense that you as parents are well pleased with him or her.

The Spartans' rite prepared their boys to be warriors— or to die trying. The Maasai prepare their boys to become men who defend their families, their herds, and their way of life. Jews mark the time that a child is considered accountable to God and His commandments, and therefore are also eligible for certain rights and responsibilities of adulthood. Significantly, the bar or bat mitzvah receives a blessing from their father, a sense that he calls down God's well-being and protection on them as they enter the world.

A personal blessing can be very powerful. As Brian Molitor, author of *Boy's Passage, Man's Journey*, writes:

> In the deepest sense, we bless someone when we speak words of encouragement and affirmation to him or her. To consider that our words can actually be used to set our sons and daughters apart for holy purposes is truly awesome. A timely, well-chosen word from a parent can encourage, enlighten, strengthen, and safeguard a child against the assaults against him or her that will inevitably come.[3]

Two

DEVELOPING THE IDEA

The boys of Sparta and Massai, and the modern bar and bat mitzvah ceremonies for Jewish boys and girls offered me helpful illustrations of rites of passage. From these cultural examples and other material I've read, I began to develop a rite of passage for my own children that would begin with *separation*, include a time of *transition*, and conclude with *incorporation*. Finally and most importantly, I wanted the rite to end with a sense of spiritual mission and a father's blessing with a unique Christian emphasis.

Through such rites, your and my children are able to feel they belong to something larger than themselves. That's a need all our sons and daughters have. Your children's rite of passage prepares them to recognize they are men and women with purpose and mission.

For me, I realized my boys would need to symbolically separate from me for a time, and that time would need a sense of adventure—but without the danger of a Spartan spear or a lion's claws! They would need a process of transition, the sense that they were moving from one thing to another, and there needed to be a learning process along the way—just as the Spartan and Maasai boys learned skills to help them survive not just the rite but their future lives in those cultures. The rite would need to end with a ceremony of incorporation, where they would be welcomed back and ushered into a larger "family" that would include not just their parents or siblings but also a group of men who would be their mentors and accountability partners, not just for a time, but for their whole lives.

Finding the Participants

I wanted to set a specific date and time when I would recognize my boys as men in their father's eyes. I wanted to set a specific date and time when I would recognize each of my girls as women in their father's eyes. This would not be a spur-of-the-moment activity or something I just drifted into. It needed to be deliberate, with a specific plan.

For my boys, I also wanted to have a specific group of people, godly men whom Buddy and Tommy already knew and could call on for support. I wanted participation by those who had significant influence in the lives of my children, people who spoke to them spiritually—maybe a pastor, a youth pastor, a mentor, and/or an accountability-group partner. It would need to be men whom I could count on in the future when my children would need wise counseling. This last part is important: *The Enemy is always trying to isolate us.* It's his way to kill and destroy by having us listen to only our own voice and not seek counsel.

Over and over in God's Word it tells us there is wisdom in many counselors (e.g., Proverbs 11:14). God would put these men in my boys' lives to be those many counselors, to help them as iron sharpens iron (Proverbs 27:17). The only exception I ever made to that was for the grandparents, who would talk specifically about family. (That, by the way, would be a great opportunity for witnessing to the grandparents or a key older family member—say, a patriarch or matriarch. If they are not saved, this rite of passage is a great process for them to be a part of, to join us in launching our children into adulthood.)

These men would come alongside Sheila and me and advise our sons. Similarly, chosen women would come alongside our daughters with advice and comfort. Each counselor would need to be someone the children would feel comfortable going to in times of crisis and who would give them sound, spiritual advice. In short, I looked for four or five key influencers in their lives—influencers for Christ. The rite itself would be a call to live a righteous life in obedience to our Lord and would be setting them on the right path for the future, a blessing in front of others, acknowledging them and encouraging them to live their lives for Christ.

My goal was to do this for each of my children on their sixteenth birthdays. With three of the four, I was able to make that goal. (My oldest daughter, Victoria, was twenty-one when we did her rite of passage.) I don't think there's any special significance to that particular age, by the way. A child can be older or younger. In fact, you might even consider different rites for different life stages.

Marking the Milestones

The Focus on the Family book *Spiritual Milestones* recommends several points at which you can intentionally mark a milestone in a child's life, based on his or her life development. For example, in addition to a baby dedication and then baptism, the authors suggest a "preparing for adolescence" rite around the time the child turns eleven; purity vows around age thirteen; a rite of passage around age fifteen; and the child's high school graduation around age eighteen.[1]

However, I thought sixteen was significant because by the time a child has reached the age of sixteen, he or she is facing a lot of life's greatest challenges. And, at least for girls, age sixteen already has a connotation of moving on to bigger things. It's a time of Sweet Sixteen parties and, in some circles, debutante balls. You know your children best, though, and can judge best when would be the right time to commit to such a ceremony. As I said earlier, this is not intended to be a one-size-fits-all process.

Highlighting the Topics

As I began to refine the idea, I came up with six key topics around which to develop parts of the rite of passage. I recommend them to you:

- Faith
- Hope
- Love
- Purity
- Integrity
- Family

Faith

Faith carries two meanings in the Bible: The first is that of trust and reliance (Romans 3:3). The second sense is of fidelity and trustworthiness. In the Old Testament the verb "to believe" occurs only thirty times, but don't conclude that a relative lack of mention means that faith is not important in the Old

Testament. After all, the New Testament draws all its examples of faith from the lives of Old Testament believers (e.g., Romans 4:18; Hebrews 11; James 2:14), and Paul rests his doctrine of faith on the word of Habakkuk 2:4, "The righteous will live by his faith." New Testament writers, especially the apostle Paul and the writer of Hebrews, show that the faith manifested by Old Testament saints, as first mentioned in reference to Abraham, was no different from that expected of today's believers. Paul makes clear that the meaning of faith is trust in the person of Jesus, the truth of His teaching, and the redemptive work He accomplished on the cross. Faith is more than just intellectual assent to the doctrinal teachings of Christianity.

> Genuine faith is born out of knowledge of the will of God and exists only to fulfill that will. The objective of faith is the will of God. Faith is not a means of getting man's will done in heaven; it is the means of getting God's will done on earth. Faith does not put God at our beck and call; rather it puts us at His. It is for "official use only," and is operational only within the sphere of His will.[2]

A personal faith in Christ would be the most important thing to communicate to my children through this rite of passage. I commend that focus to you. It is the cornerstone upon which you should build all other parts of the rite. A personal faith means living in radical and total commitment to Christ as the Lord of one's life.

I wanted each of my children to come away from this day with an understanding that faith is not something easily lived; there are so many opportunities to drift or even to doubt. I wanted to communicate that, without faith, everything else would be much harder.

Hope

Hope is a gift of the Holy Spirit that, along with faith and love, is an essential characteristic of the Christian (1 Corinthians 13:8, 13). In the Old Testament, the word *hope* is often used in the sense of "trust" or "confidence." The New Testament speaks of hope this way, as well as in the sense of expectation and desire; it includes confidence that God will be true to His Word (Romans 15:13). And our hope of glory is in Christ and His work (Colossians 1:27; 1 Timothy 1:1).

Hope is linked with faith (Hebrews 11:1) because it depends on Jesus' resurrection (1 Corinthians 15:19). We need our children to understand this: The faith that is so important to their lives leads naturally to having this great hope that God is faithful and will, through His Word and wise counselors, be a steady guide for the journey into adulthood and beyond.

Love

The Bible tells us that love is the very nature of God (1 John 4:8, 16) and the greatest of the Christian virtues (1 Corinthians 13:13). It is essential to man's relations to God and to his fellow man (Mark 12:28–31; John 13:34–35). When the disciples asked Jesus to identify the greatest commandment, He said, "'Love the Lord your God with all your heart, and with all your soul, and with all your mind' This is the first and greatest commandment" (Matthew 22:37–38 NIV).

This ultimate expression of love, loving God with our whole being, is for us what C. S. Lewis called "Need-love," the love that leads us to cry out in desire and need for God. As he wrote in *The Four Loves*:

Every Christian would agree that a man's spiritual health is exactly proportional to his love for God. But man's love for God, from the very nature of the case, must always be very largely, and must often be entirely, a Need-love. This is obvious when we implore forgiveness for our sins or support in our tribulations. But in the long run it is perhaps even more apparent in our growing—for it ought to be growing—awareness that our whole being by its very nature is one vast need; incomplete, preparatory, empty yet cluttered, crying out for Him who can untie things that are now knotted together and tie up things that are still dangling loose. . . . And God will have it so. He addresses our Need-love: "Come unto me all ye that travail and are heavy-laden."[3]

It is the fulfillment of the law (Romans 13:8–10). Love found its supreme expression in Christ's self-sacrifice on Calvary (1 John 4:10). Of course, love has several meanings that are not fully captured by the single word in English: There's *storge*, the natural affection felt between parents and children; also *philia*, the brotherly love felt between strong friends; *eros*, the physical aspect of love, particularly sexual; and *agape*, the self-sacrificing, self-giving type of love exemplified by Christ and His sacrificial death for us but also encouraged in all Christians toward both friends and enemies.

As parents, we should desire that our children understand what it means to love another but also understand it biblically, not from what our popular culture and Hollywood tell them. I wanted my children to know about love of family, love of friends, the physical love of another sanctioned within marriage, but most importantly, the sacrificial love we are commanded to exemplify. I also wanted them to understand love as that most important virtue of desiring God, of knowing our utter helplessness and need before Him and His loving-kindness in being the object of all our faith and hope.

PARTNERS *in the* PASSAGE

MY HUSBAND AND MY KIDS, and now our grandkids, are the most special gifts that God has given me.

My prayer has always been to be a good wife and mother.
I always pray for my children. I have prayed for their salvation,
for their walk with the Lord to become stronger and stronger
every day, and for them to mature to be the godly men
(fathers) and godly women (mothers) that God created them
to be.

I think taking them through these rites of passage was
another stepping stone in their walk in their faith in Christ.
It shows them that they are not in it alone, no matter where
this life takes them or what life has to offer. There are people
in their lives who are willing to help them through the good
times as well as the hard.

They may not have fully understood everything that was
going on that special day, but I know as their faith grows and
their families grow, their individual rite of passage will become
more and more meaningful and special to them. And I pray
that when their children reach the age for the time of their
own rite of passage, it will be even more special to them as
they send their children into the world to be godly young
men and women.

One of the hardest things to do is to say, "Okay, God,
they are yours," and take your hands off. The truth is they
were always His. Our job is to teach them and guide them in
His truth. Their job is to obey. This is one thing along their life's

journey that helps them get a good, strong start into knowing who they are in Christ and how much we love them and that there are others standing in the gap for them.

—*Sheila McBride*

Purity

Purity is more than just sexual abstinence until marriage. It involves an entire lifestyle and habit of mind. We need to help our children make commitments to purity during their teen years, so they will be ready for temptations during both their teen and adult years.

There is no doubt about where God stands on the subject. The apostle Paul wrote, "Do not be deceived: neither the sexually immoral nor idolaters nor adulterers nor men who practice homosexuality, nor thieves, nor the greedy, nor drunkards, nor revilers, nor swindlers will inherit the kingdom of God" (1 Corinthians 6:9–10 ESV). He added, "The body is not meant for sexual immorality, but for the Lord, and the Lord for the body. Flee from sexual immorality. Every other sin a person commits is outside the body, but the sexually immoral person sins against his own body" (1 Corinthians 6:13, 18 ESV). The New Testament contains many other warnings against engaging in sexual immorality (Galatians 5:19–21; 1 Thessalonians 4:3–5; Ephesians 5:1–3, 5). And in our sex-obsessed world, it takes more than our best efforts to maintain sexual purity. It takes the redeeming and sanctifying work of God in our lives.

Remember, your child's sexual purity involves more than just their sexual behavior. What they allow into their minds, what thoughts they dwell on, the images they view, and the words they hear all influence them. Sexual purity involves what they read, what movies and TV they watch, what music they listen to, what conversations they listen to or take part in. As the apostle Paul tells all followers of Christ, "Therefore come out from them and be separate, says the Lord. Touch no unclean thing, and I will receive you" (2 Corinthians 6:17 NIV, echoing Isaiah 52:11). But today's society is obsessed with sex and has become increasingly tolerant of sexual expression in all its forms. Followers of Christ, on the other hand, are called to be a holy people, to live lives that set us apart from the world, keeping apart from the unclean things.

The psalmist says, "I will set no worthless thing before my eyes" (Psalm 101:3). I wanted to find someone who could speak to my children about purity as a lifestyle, as a habit of mind, as something that pleases God, not just in the physical, sexual sense, but also in how they live their everyday lives. Purity is about being pure in word and deed, which leads to the next topic.

Integrity

Integrity is based on truth, not just in the sense of something being factually true, but also true in the sense of being straight and trustworthy. When Moses (Exodus 18:21) refers to "able men who fear God, men of truth, those who hate dishonest gain," he's talking about integrity of character—a kind of reliability and personal behavior that imply a love of truth, truth derived from the character of God (Hebrews 6:18; 2 Timothy 2:13; Titus 1:2). Integrity also implies being whole and sound, able to function as designed, as in, "The engineers testify to the integrity of the bridge." The bridge's integrity means it is strong and won't fall down. The same type of integrity can be applied to people: a love of truth, trustworthiness, being a man or woman of their word, functioning as

God would have us function—as a bridge functions as the engineers would have it function.

Pastor and author Warren Wiersbe describes the man and woman of integrity this way: "A person with integrity is not divided (that's duplicity) or merely pretending (that's hypocrisy). He or she is 'whole'; life is 'put together', harmoniously. People with integrity have nothing to hide and nothing to fear. Their lives are open books. They are integers."[4]

Integrity is a whole-life pursuit. We need to prepare our children for this walk—a walk of consistency that will affect every area of their lives. Even before the rite of passage, we as parents can model this walk. That means showing integrity in every area of our lives. I cannot show integrity as a businessman and then come home and lie to my wife and children. I cannot be forthright with my family and then lie to my friends. The character trait and habit of mind that would lead me to show a lack of integrity in one thing would naturally bleed over into other areas of life. I cannot be a liar at work and somehow expect to mentally shift gears and become a straight shooter at home or at church.

For that reason, during the rite I wanted to communicate to my children that being a man or woman of integrity is a full-time job and would count toward much as they enter the world of adulthood. Even though we see so many people with no integrity who seem to do well (Jeremiah 12:1), having integrity is its own reward and pleases God.

As your rite reminds them about integrity, be sure they know that integrity lost is hard to regain. Better to never lose it in the first place. But to not lose it, they need to understand what it is and how to guard it.

Family

For their rite of passage, I wanted my children to know the importance of being part of a family. Family is where we are raised, where we often can be introduced to godly living and raised in the truth of God's Word. Your relationships with your parents and siblings are different from those you have with friends, classmates, or coworkers. I've heard family described as "where they always have to take you in." You can cease to be friends with someone, classmates graduate and move on, and coworkers leave for other jobs, but your father will always be your father and your brother will always be your brother.

Family is also a picture of the relationship between God and His people. In the Old Testament, the relationship between God and Israel is seen in such family terms as "bride" (Jeremiah 2:2 NIV), "daughter" (Jeremiah 31:22), "children" (Jeremiah 3:14 ESV), or "betroth" (Hosea 2:19). The New Testament uses bridal imagery to describe the relationship between Christ and the church (2 Corinthians 11:2; Ephesians 5:25–33; Revelation 19:7; 21:9), and the church is referred to as the household of God (Galatians 6:10; Ephesians 2:19; 3:15; 1 Peter 4:17).

A lot of the problems in our world come from the fragmentation of the family. Easy divorce and multiple marriages have children bouncing from one home to the next, and sometimes competing loyalties between parents leave the child hurt and confused. I realize that some readers of this book have probably gone through a divorce and perhaps have remarried. I don't mean to condemn, as I understand many times in this age of no-fault separation that a spouse can find himself or herself divorced without wanting to. I realize also that for some that was their life before they came to Christ, and now they want to make good. No matter what your circumstances, if you're reading this book, understand that my most important message is that it's never too late. (See the last chapter for a great story on that.)

When it is time for your child's rite of passage, remember that the family portion of the rite can be performed only by someone within the family: a grandparent, parent, aunt, uncle, or perhaps an older sibling. In our case, I knew my father would be the right man for the task. I wanted to communicate what it meant to be a McBride, to talk about the family history, the legacy of the family, and the importance of understanding that they are links in the family heritage, for good or ill, and it was important to make sure they were strong links to continue the McBride name.

Final Preparation

This rite should take place in a special environment, a setting that is unique. For our children, it consisted of several stops, or "stations," where they would meet a different adult mentor, who would address one of the chosen topics. For the boys I wanted to add a bit of adventure during the separation phase, so I looked for a trail through the woods. For the girls I looked for a trip through the interior of our church, including the altar, where one day they might be married and start their families. I wanted to have them take away from that special experience, through each person they talked to, spiritual characteristics for their lives as well as a gift at each station that would remind them of that important day with its commitments and challenges.

At each station they would be learning things that would help them transition from being young men and women to adults. Both events would end up at a nice, formal luncheon, the incorporation phase where they would be symbolically reunited with their families but also welcomed into a fellow-ship of lifelong mentors.

Finding Special Men

I thought of men the boys and I knew who could speak to them about each of these topics. I recommend not telling your child much about the event ahead of time. As I was planning and praying for the first rite, I never mentioned anything to Buddy, my oldest son. The only preparation he got was being told to schedule time for the event on a Saturday morning in the near future.

The secrecy is important: I think there is something special for all of us when we realize that someone has done a whole lot of planning to do something special for us. Bringing in the mentors was part of that calculation. In the end, the kids realized, "Hey, there are people here who drove a long way to be here for this time with me, there are people who flew in to be a part of this, and this didn't just come together this morning. There was a lot of planning that has gone into preparing this event for me today." That makes the event all the more special.

Ideally the mentors you choose should all have been involved at some point in your child's life. For Buddy, I chose a football coach, a youth pastor, an uncle, a grandfather. I talked with each participant in advance to see if he had a passion or felt he had a message on one of the selected topics and asked him to pray about the specific message for my son. For your children, perhaps a favorite teacher, an older brother or sister, or a Bible-study leader would make good mentors. The important thing to consider is the relationship the mentor already has with the child and the likelihood that this person would be able or even wish to be available to provide wise counsel in the future.

Finding Unique Gifts

With a topic assigned to each man, we looked at gifts for each of those topics. The gifts should be important reminders of God's faithfulness and help. They become a form of Ebenezer—memorial stones, of sorts, things that they would hold on to and they would cherish and remember. In 1 Samuel 7:12, Samuel placed a large stone at the spot somewhere between Mizpah and Shen, where God had delivered victory over the Philistines—a place where twice earlier the Israelites had been routed by the same enemy. That stone would serve as a marker and permanent reminder of God's help. Samuel called it Ebenezer, meaning "stone of help." As my children went on through life, I hoped they would look back at the gifts and remember the message and be able to reflect on how it had helped them become better adults.

The gifts were directly tied to the topic. For example, the speaker on integrity would give a Bible. He would talk about being a man of integrity and how you can't be a man of integrity without the Word of God. For faith there was a print-out of a shield that had quotes about faith. For the family station my father would give a family heirloom, something that had belonged to his grandfather or his great-grandfather. The subject of purity called for a purity ring. As a wedding ring symbolizes the marriage bond between a husband and wife, a purity ring symbolizes the wearer's status as not yet married but remaining sexually pure for his or her future spouse. Again, you might have different ideas for appropriate gifts, things that are unique to your family or to your child. Use your imagination, and brainstorm with your spouse as the two of you pray through the planning of your child's rite of passage event. The important thing is that the gift is meaningful and appropriate to serve as a lifelong reminder of the event and the lesson.

After the main event, I planned for all of us to go somewhere for a meal to share a time of fellowship, but it was also when I would present the final gift—from me. It would be a summary of all that had gone before on that day and a remembrance, an Ebenezer for the rest of their lives. While I stress flexibility in planning your child's rite of passage, I do believe strongly that some sort of meal or other time of relaxing fellowship should be a part of wrapping up the process. First, it's just fun. Second, I believe it provides a forum for everyone who has contributed to the rite to be together to share experiences and insights and, as a body, to commemorate the occasion and commission the young man and woman.

At the meal, I planned to give each of my boys the final, key gift: a sword as a reminder that their only true weapon in the inevitable spiritual battles they would face would be the Sword of the Spirit, which is the Word of God (Ephesians 6:17). (Besides, I don't know too many boys who object to being given a real sword!) For the girls, it would be a crown, as a noble wife is a crown to her husband (Proverbs 12:4). (It would also signify their status as my special princesses!)

And I had thought about the blessing I would pray over them. This would be an original prayer based on Psalm 1:1–3 and Psalm 37:3–4. You can see how this worked during the rite of passage for our older son, Buddy, in the next chapter. As part of the blessing, I prayed that as Buddy delighted in pleasing God and His Word he would flourish as a tree planted by the waters and have a fruitful life.

John Trent and Gary Smalley's classic *The Blessing* includes many examples of blessings you can use. It's important that you give a genuine, heartfelt prayer, based on the Scripture and what you feel in your heart. Have the meal, with conversation, then clear the table, affirm each participant, let the child make the commitment, give a key gift, and then have everyone pray for the child individually. Finally, you as the parent pray a blessing.

For me, the only thing left to do was make final preparations for the first rite of passage with my eldest son, Buddy.

Three

BUDDY'S
RITE OF PASSAGE

My son Buddy was sixteen, and I believed the time was right for him. I blocked out a Saturday, invited the men I wanted to participate, and got the topics and the gifts lined up. Then I gave them the lay of the land and a little description of where they were going to be.

That morning I stationed the key men in Buddy's life in the woods along the trail at Darton College, our local community college. On the front side I shared with them the purpose of the day—what I was trying to accomplish. I stressed that this was first and foremost a *Christian* rite of passage and that they were to provide godly counsel. For this first rite I had assigned the topic to each man, although I left it up to them to get alone with God to seek wisdom and direction for their conversation with my son. I also chose the gifts to give at each station, although I would change that a bit for future rites with my other children. Even though I didn't give any kind of time limit, it worked out that each man took about fifteen or twenty minutes at his station, talking to Buddy and praying with him about their given topic.

I had told Buddy to prepare to spend a Saturday doing something special with me. Until this point, he still had no idea what was going to happen. One reason I did it this way was that I wanted to see his expression when he realized that all these people had come in from out of town just to be a part of this event in his life. I know some people who spend a year lining up the event, preparing the child. But I think there is something special and significant when all of a sudden one realizes that someone has done a considerable amount of planning for something where the focus is on you. I told Buddy, "Hey, I want to hang out with you this coming Saturday, so don't plan anything. We'll be together much of the day. We need to leave home about 8:45 a.m." I had planned to start the rite at 9 a.m.

We drove around a bit, and then I took us over to where the walking trail begins. I parked and said, "Let's walk up this trail for a few minutes." He was getting a little suspicious. Once on the trail, where it enters the woods, I stopped and told him, "Today is the day that I have set aside for you as a rite of passage, recognizing your transition to manhood. I, as your dad, am recognizing you as a man in my eyes."

I told him that today was the day when the little boy would sit down and a man would stand up. Today was going to be a special time for him, a time for me and others to acknowledge what God was doing in his life and to challenge him for the days ahead. I prayed a simple prayer, and I asked him to follow the trail where he would see and hear from others along the way.

PARTNERS *in the* PASSAGE

I DIDN'T REALLY KNOW what to think. Dad kind of explained it to me, but he was trying to keep it kind of secretive and not really say too much, which at the time I didn't like. I don't like surprises; I like to know everything that is going to happen.   —*Buddy McBride*

"I have set aside a special time and ceremony to highlight this moment in your life," I explained. "I want you to walk down this trail. You will run into some men you know. I want you to capture and think about the things that they say to you at each point. All you have to do is walk down the trail and you will get your instructions from them."

Then I prayed for him and sent him walking the trail.

Keith on Purity

When he got inside the tree line, the first person he encountered was his youth pastor, Keith Harmon. Buddy had known Keith for years and had been active in his youth group at church. I knew Keith and trusted him and, more important, I knew that Buddy knew and trusted Keith. I had asked Keith to talk to him about purity, not just sexual purity, but purity in every area of Buddy's life.

Keith shared with Buddy from 1 Corinthians 6:19 (NIV). It says, "Do you not know that your body is a temple of the Holy Spirit, who is in you, whom you have received from God? You are not your own." We live in a culture that tells us if it feels good, it must be right. Our society places a high value on autonomy, which can be a good thing, but not when it leads us to think that we can do anything we like so long as it doesn't hurt someone else. I wanted Buddy to know that if you claim the name of Christ, you are not your own. You have been bought for a price, and you owe it to your new "owner" to take care of His "property."

PARTNERS *in the* PASSAGE

WHEN JIM TOLD ME about it, I immediately got very excited. I was excited for Jim and for the boys, but I was excited about the concept of doing something like that—very specific, very intentional—to hand down some of those traits that me and my family value and are important for young men as they try to go from being a boy to being a young man. . . . That was definitely something that I could pass on to Buddy, because that was done for me.

I talked about how his body was not his own. As Christians our bodies are the temple of the Holy Spirit and they have been bought with a price. To be a Christian is more than just words. To remain sexually pure is more than just being a virgin when you get married. It is a lifestyle. It is what you allow into your eyes; it is what you allow into your ears. It's what you do when you are on a date or what you don't do, but it's so much more than that.   —*Keith Harmon*

What a great lesson! Keith hit all the points about purity that I thought were important, and this lesson coming from someone Buddy respected meant all that much more.

After Keith talked with Buddy about purity, he gave him a purity ring that had Job 31:1 engraved on the inside of it. He put the ring on Buddy's finger and prayed with him before sending him down the trail.

Jimmy on Integrity

The next person he came upon was his head football coach, Jimmy Fields. As with Keith, I had known Jimmy for a long time; he used to coach the team at our church's high school, Sherwood Christian Academy. He was a good coach, and he was tough. But I respected him, and more important, Buddy respected him. He was just the person to talk to Buddy about integrity.

Jimmy walks with integrity. He works hard, he plays hard, and he prays hard. He talked about what it means to be a man of integrity. He talked about the fact that you cannot be a man of integrity without the Word of God and why he needs to mediate on it day and night. As I said earlier, integrity is what holds all the rest together, and once lost, it's hard to get back.

PARTNERS *in the* PASSAGE

I HADN'T REALLY HEARD of anything detailed like this, and I was obviously intrigued, my interest being in any church mentoring, whether it be young boys or men. I had a combination of excitement and fear—excited because I think whether you are a coach or a pastor or maybe just a guy who sells insurance, there is a natural comradeship among men, as there should be. At the same time I think there was a healthy fear. I didn't want to drop the ball here; I hoped God would be able to speak through me.

I told Buddy that your character is what you do when no one is looking. I told him that as he grew older and gained more independence, there were going to be more opportunities where it may appear that no one is looking, but obviously God is always looking into our hearts. With that newfound independence, he would have more responsibility as he is growing into a young man. I shared with Buddy that everyday integrity can't be something that you just talk about at a ceremony or a rite of passage; it has to become part of you, putting right into practice, of drawing those boundaries, allowing God's Holy Spirit through His Word to draw those lines for you every day. It is not optional.   *—Jimmy Fields*

Again, a great lesson delivered by someone Buddy respected. He'd also see the lesson lived out in the way Coach Fields lived his life and coached the football team. Jimmy finished, prayed with Buddy, and gave him a Bible that was signed by all the guys who were on the trail that day. He then sent him on down the trail.

Andy on Faith

The next person he ran into was his uncle Andy Baker. Andy talked to him about faith and what it meant to be a man of faith.

To my boys, Andy is the "fun uncle." They do things with him that they don't normally get to do at home. But Andy is also great at imparting lessons, and he was the perfect person to talk to Buddy about faith. When my boys, Buddy and Tommy, were younger, Sheila and I would often send them to spend some summer vacations at their Uncle Andy's in Alabama. One of those summers, when Buddy and Andy stopped at a store, they got an unexpected chance to learn a life lesson.

As Andy recalls, "We stopped at a gas station to get a drink. On the way out, I noticed that Buddy was unwrapping a piece of candy. Knowing that I didn't pay for it when the cashier rang up our sodas, I assumed that Buddy had just taken it. Shocked, I scolded him and whacked him right there. Today, Buddy jokingly says that I scared him for life. I think that may be true in a good way because I doubt if he has ever taken anything without paying again."

Uncle Andy later got an opportunity to learn a valuable lesson about being overconfident, when Buddy and Tommy went to spend some time with him in North Carolina. It was a potentially dangerous state of affairs, and just like the first time, it was Andy who wound up learning the more important lesson. As Andy recalls, "I had the boys over, and I knew they were nosy and might find the .38 pistol I kept in my drawer for protection. It's a semiautomatic, and I would store it with the magazine in it. I showed them the proper procedure for clearing the weapon and making sure it was safe.

"After I showed them this, I put the magazine in, let the carriage go forward, and then aimed it at the wall, thinking it would go click. Well, it didn't go click. It went BANG.

"I tell you, I've been around guns all my life. But I've had nightmares just thinking how confident I was in myself. If the thought had crossed my mind, I might have aimed it at the dog or, God forbid, one of them and pulled the trigger, and that would have been really bad. So when Jim asked me to talk to Buddy, I wondered what was I going to talk to him about. I was thinking it would be forgiveness or encouragement or some particular thing.

"I brought with me on our walk a piece of candy and a bullet. We talked about mistakes we have made and how we move on from our mistakes" (see "Partners in the Passage" for more from Andy).

PARTNERS *in the* PASSAGE

I THOUGHT IT WAS a pretty neat idea. I was honored to be asked, although I kind of jokingly called it a bar mitzvah.

[My object lesson on having faith in the right thing included] bringing a piece of candy and a bullet. I said to Buddy, "This piece of candy represents a very small mistake you made. This bullet represents a very big mistake I made that could have been worse. The moral of the story is that we move on. We make mistakes, but we move on. We forgive ourselves and others, but we certainly learn from our mistakes and try not to repeat them."   —*Andy Baker*

Andy talked about how in those instances he'd had great faith in himself and in his understanding of the situation. It turned out in both cases that his faith in himself had been misplaced. That was a great opportunity to tell Buddy that there's only one safe place to put one's faith: in God and His faithfulness. Because Buddy had lived those two lessons, I think it drove home the point even more powerfully. Andy gave Buddy a poster called "The Shield of Faith," which was a print of a shield with verses about faith on it. On the back was brown paper on which every man involved in his rite of passage had written a special message to him.

Grandpa McBride on Family

Andy prayed with Buddy and sent him on down the trail. Next he encountered his grandfather, James G. McBride Sr. His grandfather talked to him about what it meant to be a McBride man.

Grandpa McBride told him about his family heritage and about stories from his father and his father's father, stories of men of character who had come before him in his family. He gave him a pocket watch that had belonged to *his* grandfather. That watch meant a lot to my father, and it meant even more to Buddy when he received it, handed down from all those generations. It was a tangible symbol of those men who had held it, examined it, and cared for it.

PARTNERS *in the* PASSAGE

I THINK RIGHT NOW it's really important for children to realize where the family came from and how they got where they are spiritually. I think a lot of kids are missing out on the family stuff.   —*Grandpa McBride*

After all those years, the watch was now his to own and take care of, to perhaps pass on to his own son or grandson some day, just as he would own and pass on the McBride name and everything that had gone with it over the past generations.

The Rendezvous and Lunch

As Buddy traveled down the trail, each man walked back the way Buddy had come and met me at the beginning of the trail. Once Grandpa McBride was finished, he prayed with Buddy and then walked him back out of the trail, where he met up with all the guys who'd had a part in this special day.

We all took a few moments just to catch up and for Buddy to talk about the experience. Then we loaded up and went to a local restaurant for lunch. There was no set agenda for the meal portion—just conversation and fellowship. Buddy sat with ears tuned as he listened to the men of different generations talk about the day-to-day things that were happening in their lives and in their world. He was like a sponge, soaking it up, hearing what these men, whom he respected so much, had to say. That's a sure sign you've picked the right people.

As soon as the lunch dishes were cleared, I stood up on one side of the table, next to Buddy. (We were in a semiprivate section of the restaurant.) I thanked each man who had been part of the journey, and I affirmed each of them in front of my son. I said, "Keith, I appreciate the prayer warrior you have been for me and the way you have always given me wise counsel when I've sought the Lord on something and how you have been an encouragement to me. I want to thank you for that. I want to ask you today if you would stand and look my son in the eye and make that kind of commitment to him, to be that kind of godly counselor, prayer supporter, and encourager for him."

Then he stood and looked Buddy in the eye and made that commitment. Keith remained standing. I turned to the next guy and worked my way around the room, affirming them in front of my son, thanking them, highlighting spiritual things they'd done in my life and then asking them if they would make the commitment to be that kind of encourager and spiritual counsel for Buddy that they had been for me.

By the time I worked my way around, everybody in the room was standing except for my son. Then I said, "Buddy, there is a point in every young man's life when a boy sits down but a man stands up, and this is that moment for you. Here stand a group of men who are close to you, who love you, who have committed to pray for you, encourage you, and be a resource for you when you are seeking godly wisdom. Today I am asking you, will you stand up as a man, and look these men back in the eye and promise that when you come to those moments in your life, rather than succumbing to the attack of the enemy, you will seek the Lord for godly counsel and that you will take them up on this commitment they have made to you? To pray for you and make themselves available to give you counsel."

Preparing Buddy for Battle

Buddy stood up and looked them in the eye and made that commitment. After everyone was seated again, I talked about our family. We are of Scottish background. I talked to him about the movie *Braveheart* and the story of William Wallace, dubbed "Guardian of Scotland and Leader of its armies" for his fight for freedom for the Scots from the despotic English king Edward I, also called Edward Longshanks for his great height. I said that our family back in Scotland could have fought with William Wallace. I told Buddy that he may never have to fight a physical battle such as the men in *Braveheart*, but as long he lived he would be in a spiritual battle. The only offensive weapon he has for that battle is the Word of God.

Then I reached down and pulled out a William Wallace–type sword and laid it out before him. (You can find replicas on the Internet or at gift or trophy shops.) It was the Scottish Claymore, a two-handed broadsword (forty-six inches long!) that was in common use during the time of William Wallace. I'd had engraved on it the names of the men who took part in his rite of passage and also the date.

I said, "Buddy, this is a replica of the sword that William Wallace carried. If you notice, on one side of the blade are the names of six men, including me, who are here today as part of this event." I flipped it over. "On the other side is your name and this date, May 12, 2002, as a memorial to what's happened here today. I want you to hang this on the wall at the foot of your bed so you will be reminded every morning when you wake up and when you go to bed of the weapon you have against the enemy—the Word of God. I want you to wear the ring of purity that Keith gave you and live a life of purity before the Lord. I want you to take up the shield of faith your Uncle Andy gave you as the defensive weapon that will shield you from every fiery dart fired by the enemy. I want you to live a life of integrity like Coach Fields talked to you about by using, learning, and loving the Word of God. I want you to be a man of character and integrity, like your grandpa talked to you about."

A Time to Pray

After that, the men all gathered around Buddy, and each took a moment to pray for him. I finished by praying a spiritual blessing over him as his father, using verses out of Psalm 1 and Psalm 37 along with personal blessings and affirmations of God's gifting in his life.

Blessed is the man who does not walk in the counsel of the wicked, nor stand in the path of sinners, nor sit in the seat of scoffers! But his delight is in the law of the Lord, and in His law he meditates day and night. He will be like a tree firmly planted by streams of water, which yields its fruit in its season and its leaf does not wither; and in whatever he does, he prospers. (Psalm 1:1–3)

Delight yourself in the Lord, and he will give you the desires of your heart. Commit your way to the Lord; trust in him, and he will act. He will bring forth your righteousness as the light, and your justice as the noonday. (Psalm 37:4–6 ESV)

When I was finished, we gathered together and took pictures of Buddy with the sword, with all the men surrounding him, and with each man who had participated in his special day.

And with that I had finished my first rite of passage. It was as moving and meaningful to me as I know it was to Buddy. And that meant only one thing: I would have to do the same or better for Tommy.

Four

TOMMY'S
TURN

W hen it came time to perform the second rite
of passage with my other son, Tommy, I had refined
the idea a bit and made some changes. I added a speaker, and
I fine-tuned the ideas that I wanted each man to talk about.
Chief among the changes was that I asked each man what he
felt led to talk about, and I let each man choose the gift he
thought best for his topic. The only gift I said Tommy must be
given was a Bible, as had been given to Buddy, and I intended
to give Tommy a sword similar to Buddy's.

On May 13, 2004, I woke Tommy up and asked him to go
for a ride. Again, I had placed men in position along the trail at
Darton College. Because of what we'd done with Buddy two
years earlier, Tommy knew this was the day for his rite of passage. He knew something was going to happen. After all, Buddy
had put this big ol' sword over his bed, and even though Tommy
didn't know all the details, he had some idea something was

going to happen. He had no idea, however, who was in the woods prepared to meet him or what they might say.

Once we began our walk along the Darton trail, I told Tommy that today was his rite of passage, a day when he would pass from being a boy to being a man. It was a day when men he knew had gathered to help signify that time in his life. As I had done with Buddy, I told him that this was a special day to mark his becoming a man. I prayed with him and then encouraged him to walk down the trail, where others would meet him along the way.

PARTNERS *in the* PASSAGE

FOR ME THE RITE OF PASSAGE was not an event or a birthday present. It was a call to responsibility. I believe the reason why young people are not doing great things is because they are not given great responsibility.

The reason I embraced the principles of my rite of passage is because my father prepared me for it. This preparation did not consist of a rundown of the day's events or lecture on why it was important. It was by seeing my parents live out these principles in their relationship with each other and their relationship with Christ on a daily basis.

—*Tommy McBride*

Keith's Words

The first person to meet him, as with Buddy, was Keith Harmon, his former youth pastor. Keith talked to him about what it meant to live a life of purity. He used the Scripture

Job 31:1, "I made a covenant with my eyes not to look lustfully at a woman." He talked to him about being pure in every area of his life, not just sexually, although being sexually pure until marriage is what God demands of those who follow Him. But Keith told Tommy that he was to pursue purity in his thought life, purity in choices of entertainment, what he chose to read, what he allowed into his mind. Purity was not a part-time job; he had to be on guard full time against anything that might cause his mind to go astray. He gave Tommy a purity ring to wear with the Job verse engraved inside.

PARTNERS *in the* PASSAGE

I THOUGHT BOTH BOYS received it very well. Part of that is that both of them were very good boys; it's not like it was the first time they had heard what I had to say. Their mom and dad poured those values into them from an early age. I had a relationship with them. It wasn't a stranger just randomly talking with them but rather somebody they had a very good relationship with already. Not all of those conversations with students go so well because sometimes I am saying something different than what their lifestyle has taught them or even what a mom or dad has modeled for them. Sometimes those are very difficult conversations to have, but with both of those guys I know that it wasn't the first time they heard that. It was probably the thousandth time they heard that.   —*Keith Harmon*

Like Buddy, Tommy received a purity ring made of silver. Although Keith presented the ring, as his father I paid for it. Such rings typically cost fifty to seventy dollars. Many Christian bookstores and some of their websites carry these rings. It's a special ring, a reminder your son will wear until his wedding day, when he will exchange it for a wedding band, when he pledges to remain faithful to his beloved.

Keith prayed with Tommy, prayed to keep his heart and mind pure, and then encouraged him to continue down the trail.

Coach Fields Returns

The next person on the trail was his head football coach from Sherwood Christian Academy, Jimmy Fields. Jimmy's experience with Tommy was different from what he'd had with Buddy. He knew both boys well, and he knew each had a different temperament, a different way of interacting with others. While Buddy is quiet and reserved, Tommy is more outgoing. Coach Fields knew that, and that's why it's so important to pick men who know your boys, who have taught them or coached them or been around them for some time. Because of this, Coach Fields was able to tailor his approach to each boy to suit his personality and temperament.

PARTNERS *in the* PASSAGE

WHEN TOMMY'S TURN rolled around, even though I had been part of it before, it still took on new meaning. They are brothers, but they are two different individuals. I was very sensitive to knowing that God has very specific purposes and plans for each boy, not photocopies for each of us. I was sensitive to knowing that those plans God had for Buddy

several years earlier were not necessarily the plans that God
had for Tommy. They were unique and different.

—Jimmy Fields

Jimmy Fields gave Tommy a Bible that had been signed by
every man who was participating that day. As he'd done with
Buddy, Jimmy talked to him about what it meant to be a man
of integrity. He explained that it is impossible to be a man of
integrity without the Word of God.

This was not the first time Jimmy had emphasized integrity
to Tommy. "One thing that Coach Fields has always talked
about, the one thing he has instilled in me and in the other
football players was being a man of integrity," Tommy said.
"Integrity was always the biggest thing for him." So it was natural to have the coach meet him on that trail.

He prayed with Tommy and encouraged him to walk on
down the trail.

A Gift from Andy and Radio

It was now time for Tommy to meet some family members.
He soon spotted his Uncle Andy, who spoke about what it
meant to be a man of love.

I had contacted Andy two months before the date, and
Andy wondered how he could explain a lived-out love—the
agape, sacrificial love we find in the Bible. Andy decided to visit
the campus of T. L. Hanna High School in Anderson, South
Carolina, the school where the man affectionately known as
Radio works and serves the football team. His life became the
subject of the movie *Radio*. It's the true story of how Coach

Harold Jones showed real, sacrificial love to a developmentally disabled man, James "Radio" Kennedy, who loved to hang out with the high school football team. At some potential sacrifice to his job, Coach Jones took Radio under his wing.

Radio got his nickname from the beat-up old radio he always carried with him. Because of his disability he was an object of derision by the players and many at the school, and because of a bad misunderstanding, the school threatened to ban Radio from the one thing he loved most: Hanna High School and its football games.

Coach Jones's commitment to Radio meant that he was willing to give up the job he loved out of love for Radio but also out of love for a principle—a very biblical principle, even if the movie never explicitly says so. In the process, he shows us not only his love for Radio, but Radio's love for people who treat him poorly. In the movie, Coach Jones puts it this way, addressing the high school booster club:

> I love football. I love everything about it. I love Friday nights when you're looking for a win and Saturday morning when you've found one. But that's not what's important right now. We got ourselves a young man we're not thinking about. The same young man. . . who got himself a football letter last fall but he never wears it 'cause he can't afford a jacket. Now we're asking him to leave. I know some of you don't know or don't care about all that Radio's learned over these past few months. But truth is, we're not the ones who've been teaching Radio. Radio is the one who's been teaching us. *'Cause the way he treats us all the time is the way we wish we treated each other even part of the time*[1] [emphasis added].

The coach's last line is the perfect embodiment of Jesus' words after he spelled out the greatest commandment, "And the second is like it: 'Love your neighbor as yourself'" (Matthew 22:39). Eventually, through that coach's efforts, the town and school came to adopt Radio and made him their own. That coach's love for someone who was considered unlovable made a huge difference in everyone's lives.

PARTNERS *in the* PASSAGE

I TALKED WITH TOMMY about how this football coach had offered love to someone who a lot of society considered unlovable, and how the coach had offered unconditional love and what it meant.   —*Andy Baker*

In preparation for Tommy's rite of passage, Uncle Andy traveled to Hanna High, where Radio still works with the same football team. There they had a picture taken together, and Radio signed a football. Andy created a plaque with the photo and football, with the words, "Love conquers all." Andy talked to Tommy about God's love and about how God's love conquers all.

That gift was very meaningful for Tommy, both as a young man and as a football player. Andy prayed with Tommy and sent him on down the trail.

Words from Two Grandfathers

Next to meet Tommy on the trail was Harry McKinney, his step-grandfather; he has long been involved and influential in Tommy's life. Harry talked about what it meant to be a man of faith. Like me, Grandpa Harry is a former Marine, and he shared the legacy of honor, courage, and commitment that comes from service in the Corps.

PARTNERS *in the* PASSAGE

WITH TOMMY BEING from a strong Christian background, my first and foremost thoughts were about talking about something relating to religion as far as his adult life was concerned and furthering his education as far as anything he might be doing in his Christian walk.   —*Harry McKinney*

Harry encouraged Tommy and prayed with him and sent him farther down the trail. There his grandfather, James G. McBride Sr., was waiting. Tommy's grandfather told him about his family heritage and what it meant to be a McBride man. As with Buddy, he gave Tommy a gift of something that had been in the family a long time and that had great meaning to him. He talked to him about his father and his father's father and the character examples they had set that he had tried to emulate in his own life.

PARTNERS *in the* PASSAGE

GRANDPA McBRIDE GAVE ME some coins that belonged to my great-great-uncle Woody, and he gave me a lot of family heirlooms. I remember when he gave me those things and talked about men in our family and about my great-uncle, and then he talked about my dad and all the

things he has done for our family. He told me how proud of me
he was. I remember he started crying, which was huge,
because I've never seen him very emotional at all. I just
remember him crying and saying he loved me and how proud
of me he was. He said he was proud of the way I lived my life,
of how I was a Christian and living with integrity, and how
much it meant to him. That is probably the one that sticks
with me the most.   —*Tommy McBride*

A Rendezvous for Lunch—at Home

Grandpa McBride then sent him back out of the woods,
where all the men gathered together. From there we went back
to a private lunch at our house. The first time, with Buddy,
had been at a restaurant. By the time I got to the second, I had
realized it was better to be in privacy, in a quiet place where
you are not worried about distractions from other people,
waiters coming and going, clearing dishes, and so forth. (It was
also easier to deal with bringing a forty-six-inch blade into my
home than into a restaurant!) Tommy's mother and some of
the other women involved in the men's lives prepared the
lunch and had it all ready for us by the time got there.

Whether you host the luncheon at home or at a local restaurant, be sure you have privacy. You don't want distractions
during the presentation; it's an intimate, personal occasion. If you
meet at a restaurant, you need a private room. For Buddy the
room was only a semiprivate area, and afterward I knew I wanted
to be at home for the next rite of passage. A home feels more
family-centered. You can go to a restaurant with a private room,
though I recommend you have the meal at a home.

As with Buddy, the men shared around the table, talking about life, about things that were going on in the world. However, this time Tommy's brother, Buddy, joined the meal. He shared some of his experiences with the rite itself and what had happened in his life since. Tommy listened and absorbed, taking in all the knowledge and counsel that was going on around the table. Clearly I had selected *the right mentors*, a crucial element in planning your child's rite of passage.

PARTNERS *in the* PASSAGE

ALL MY LIFE all these people had been teaching me, like a youth minister teaching me things of the church, or my football coach teaching me to play football. Meanwhile, my parents never had to say "I taught you better than that," because they showed me better than that. That's why the greatest honor for me next to being like my heavenly Father is to be like my earthly father.   —*Tommy McBride*

Swords Together

When we were finished eating, and after the table was cleared, I talked with Tommy, as I had with Buddy, about the fact that there was a good chance that our Scottish family may have fought alongside the great freedom fighter William Wallace. I reminded him that he may never have to fight a physical battle, but that as long as he lives he would have to fight a spiritual battle.

I asked his brother, Buddy, to present Tommy with his own William Wallace broadsword. Engraved on one side were

Tommy's name and the date, May 13, 2004. Engraved on the other side were the names of all the men who were participating that day. Buddy presented him with the sword and then picked up his own sword. The two boys were seated to my left and to my right as I sat at the head of the table. At this point they crossed their swords, and I reached out and grabbed the blades together carefully and looked them both in the eye.

As I looked at Tommy, I asked him to mount this sword in his room in a place where every morning as he arose he could be reminded of the sword of the Spirit, the Word of God, the only offensive weapon that he has against the enemy. With their swords now locked together, I told Tommy and Buddy that as a father and two sons, we would be as Ecclesiastes 4:12 says, "a cord of three strands [that] is not quickly torn apart." My prayer for them was that, as a band of brothers, we would be so knit together that we would always love, honor, and support one another, coming to one another's aid in times of trouble, praying for each other, and as iron sharpens iron, we would sharpen each other and strengthen each other as we grew more and more into the image of our Lord and Savior, Jesus Christ.

Then Buddy and Tommy each sat down with their swords, and I told Tommy that when those times of crisis came, I wanted him to take up that sword of the Spirit and to wield it and rest upon the Word of God. I reminded him to take up the shield of faith that his grandfather had talked to him about, to live that life of purity that his youth pastor had spoken of, and to be a man of integrity as his football coach had talked to him about. I also asked him to remember the heritage of the men who had gone before him.

As I had for Buddy, I then asked each of the men if they would make a personal commitment to become Tommy's counselor and prayer warrior throughout the days of his life.

They did. Then as Tommy sat in a chair, separate and apart in the room, we gathered around him and each man prayed for him.

Again, as with Buddy, after each man had prayed, I laid hands on his head and prayed a special blessing from Psalm 1 and Psalm 37. When we were finished praying, we took pictures of the group, of Tommy and his sword, and of Tommy and his brother together with their swords.

At first I thought I might be finished with rites of passage for my family, but of course I have two daughters, and the germ of an idea of doing something special for them had started to grow.

Five

VICTORIA'S RITE

Soon after the rite for my second son, Sheila and I talked about the fact that I hadn't done a rite of passage for our daughters. I came to believe that a rite of passage is not just something a father does with his son; it should be something a father does with all his *children*. The same issues of walking in faith, hope, love, purity, integrity, and guarding your heart in Christ Jesus are just as important for our girls. I wanted them to hear from their father that they had my blessing and that I loved them and was setting them up with the same kind of counsel as their brothers.

If you have daughters, I trust you can see the benefits as well. In *Girl's Passage, Father's Duty*, Brian and Kathleen Molitor explain the importance of a girl's rite of passage, of offering mentoring, blessing, and prayers:

> A daughter who receives her dad's love, time, and attention generally fares well in this life. Conversely, daughters

deprived of their father's love, time, and attention are left vulnerable to a wide variety of attacks. This exposure obviously exists in homes where the dad is absent; however, it is also present in houses where a father lives under the same roof yet fails to provide mentoring, words of blessing, healing touch, and prayers for his children.

We must acknowledge that our daughters' lives are not fairy tales with prewritten, happy endings. The threat against each of them is real, and the ending of the story is yet to be decided. In fact, the challenge is so great it will take a hero to save the day. A hero called . . . Father.[1]

A Different Kind of Trail

At the same time, I knew the rite had to be entirely different from the guys' ceremony. So, again, I began to seek some godly counsel, including women's counsel, speaking with my wife and praying through what this might look like. Some of the core principles would be the same—having people along the journey to talk about faith, hope, love, purity, integrity, and family—but we knew the environment had to be different for the girls. I also wanted to have the same sequence of separation, transition, and incorporation. Girls are more like princesses than warriors. For the guys, the trail, being out in the woods, was more of a big deal to them. For the girls, we looked for an environment that would speak closer to their hearts. For us that centered on home base—our church. We figured one day they would be married in a church at an altar, and you couldn't ask for a better place to talk about purity in every area of your life.

So we laid out a "trail" around our church building and grounds. First, I told my oldest daughter, Victoria, that I wanted to spend Friday with her. She was working at the church for the summer, so on that day she just thought she was going to work as usual.

I had already spoken with the women who would be involved. I had talked about their topics; they had the same topics as the guys: faith, hope, love, purity, integrity, and family. But I gave them more freedom to formulate their own thoughts on their specific subject, more so than with the boys. I told them it was important to speak about the topic, but they should feel free to add anything else the Lord placed on their heart that would be an appropriate word for a young woman.

Again, this is where picking the right people is so important. If you're going to allow the adults to "freelance" on precisely what they're going to say, be sure that they're individuals you know well and that you have a good idea about what they're going to say.

Each woman brought her own gift that symbolized what her topic meant to her. They actually came up with several unique gifts. Some of them wrote out journals; one of them, along with giving the purity ring, wrote out a page of her thoughts to give on a scroll. They were very creative.

Beginning in the Tower

We love our church; one of its greatest strengths is the prayer ministry. Its two-story Prayer Tower is a landmark and home to a 24/7 prayer ministry. The prayer warriors of Sherwood Baptist Church send as many as one thousand prayer cards a week to people all over the world as they intercede for them. Because of the significance of the Prayer Tower and the significance of prayer to our daily life as believers, I thought this would be a fitting place to start Victoria's rite of passage. I took Victoria to the outside of the Prayer Tower on the church grounds and prayed with her. I then instructed her to go to the upper room of the Prayer Tower. There she found a note asking her to call her great-aunt, Harriett Golden, who was not able to join us in person that day.

PARTNERS *in the* PASSAGE

I KNEW THAT MY DAD had performed a rite with both my brothers, but I had no idea that mine was coming. I was actually working at the church that summer, helping out in the children's area. Daddy kept insisting that I dress up and look nice one day. It was a Friday, and we normally wear jeans. I should have guessed, but still I was a little surprised. It was kind of exciting, because I wasn't really expecting it.

When I got upstairs in the tower, there was a small Bible lying on the couch. It was from my great-aunt. There was also a piece of paper telling me to call her because she couldn't be there. The Bible was for me, as I went to each place that day, to highlight and underline the main verse that each of the ladies would talk to me about. I still have that Bible.

—*Victoria McBride*

Along with the Bible, Victoria found some highlighters and a pen so she could highlight all the Scripture verses people would give her and write the person's name and the date beside all those verses. That's one thing, as I look back, that I wish I had done with my boys. I would have given them the Bible first, because it's hard to remember everything you hear, and then something with which to write. (Several of the women even wrote down what they said to Victoria to help her remember.)

Great-Aunt Harriet on Integrity

Great-aunt Harriett spoke with Victoria about what it meant to be a woman of integrity. For women, integrity involves all the attributes we expect of men, but women carry an extra burden. It is so easy for a woman to be labeled as lacking integrity for engaging in behavior for which a man wouldn't earn that label, even if that behavior is wrong for a man, too. For a woman, even the hint of impropriety can carry lasting consequences, so she has to work extra hard at living out integrity. It's not fair, but that's the way it is.

Aunt Harriett explained that you can't be a woman of integrity without the Word of God. Harriett gave the Bible to Victoria as a gift. That Bible had special significance for Harriett and was therefore very valuable to her. It had been given to Victoria's great-great-grandmother for Christmas one year by Victoria's great-grandparents. It was then given by Victoria's great-grandparents to Harriett in recognition of her salvation many years earlier. And now Harriett was giving it to Victoria in recognition of her transition from being a girl to a woman. Harriett prayed with Victoria and then instructed her to go to the next station in the church, to the altar in the main sanctuary, where she met Dee Kelley, one of her Bible teachers and a teacher at her school.

Her Teacher Dee on Purity

Dee has been a friend and a mentor to Victoria for a number of years. Dee was going to talk to Victoria about purity. As with boys and integrity, girls carry an extra burden when it comes to living out the ideal of purity. Again, in the wider culture boys can get away with things that would condemn a girl to being called a "loose woman" or the like. An unfair double-standard? Sure, but it's reality all the same.

Dee had written all she would say that day and placed it on a scroll, which she gave to Victoria. She also gave her a purity ring to wear until the day of her marriage, reminding Victoria to keep herself pure and holy. Dee explained that one day Victoria would appear before this altar or maybe another altar with the man God had given her for marriage.

PARTNERS *in the* PASSAGE

IT WAS A HUGE HONOR to be asked to participate in Victoria's rite of passage. I felt intimidated, quite frankly, by the topic. Just speaking to a young girl about purity, that is such a personal subject. How do I encourage a young lady to continue in being pure in all areas of life? I wanted to speak truth into her life. I wanted to speak not just to sexual purity, but to life purity.

Because she was young, I went to I Timothy 4:12; it was my life verse at the time. "Don't let anyone look down on you because you are young, but set an example for the believers in speech, in life, in love, in faith and in purity" (NIV). I explained to her that purity is something that God desires in all of us. It is found not just within the confines of your relationships, but it is in your speech, and it's in the example you set for people in your life and in your faith, keeping God first and foremost. It was about keeping her mind pure by hiding God's Word in her heart.   —*Dee Kelley*

Dee told her that she should come to that altar pure before a Holy God, and that ring would be a symbol of that purity. Upon marriage, she would exchange the purity ring for a wedding ring.

Aunt Sherie on Faith

After Dee prayed with Victoria, she sent her to the church's bridal suite, where she met her Aunt Sherie Baker, who talked to her about faith. (Sherie's husband, Andy, participated in both Buddy and Tommy's rites.)

The heroes of faith in Hebrews persevered for the things promised but not yet come. As Scripture says, "Now faith is the assurance of things hoped for, the conviction of things not seen. For by it the men of old gained approval" (Hebrews 11:1–2). This faith means believing and acting on something we cannot see, and the author of Hebrews commends the heroes of faith in the Old Testament for this. He's talking not so much about what faith *is*, but more about what it *looks like* by pointing to the lives of those who walked by faith: Abel and Enoch, Noah and Abraham, Isaac, Jacob, Joseph, and so many others.

As a young woman, Victoria had most of her life ahead of her, and the heroes of Hebrews 11 would provide her with real examples of others who lived lives of hope because of their faith in God.

PARTNERS *in the* PASSAGE

THROUGH PRAYER I was asking the Lord how He would want me to approach everything with Victoria so that she would be able to understand. Victoria is very mature in her knowledge of the Word. I wanted to be able to talk to her about faith at a level she would understand, then go into Scripture to show her faith, like in Hebrews. She was an example to her sister as well as to other young adults. I told her that I always had admired her because of that level of maturity.

—*Sherie Baker*

Her Aunt Sherie gave her a plaque with Scripture about faith, including Hebrews 11:6, which says faith pleases God. Then she prayed with Victoria.

Two Grandmas Speak

Aunt Sherie then sent her to the choir room, where her grandmother, my mom, Norma Jean McKinney, spoke with her about family and heritage. Victoria's grandmother gave her a handwritten book about her life and the lessons she had learned spiritually and things she had seen in her lifetime. Because of my mom's personal circumstances, she was able to wrap up several biblical lessons into one.

PARTNERS *in the* PASSAGE

JIM'S DAD AND I are divorced, but we are better friends now than we were when we were married. I wrote a journal of my life so she would realize that even though the Bible says not to divorce, we did. It was a forgivable sin. Afterwards, I prayed for a good Christian man, and Papa Harry, as they call him, came into my life. The journal I wrote for her came from the heart, and she cried and I cried. Everybody is going to make mistakes. I stressed that it was the integrity and the truth of the Bible that you went by. I can't go back and erase anything. That was what I was trying to say to her. I learned a lot through my life, and I would love to not see them have to go through the hardships.

—*Norma Jean McKinney*

Through her grandmother's example, Victoria was able to see faith, hope, love, and integrity all in action. Yes, my mom and dad made a mistake when they were younger. But if our faith means anything, it means there is forgiveness, too, and Norma Jean was a living, breathing example of someone who had been forgiven and who had hard-learned lessons to pass on to her granddaughter.

Next Victoria returned to the sanctuary, where Grandma Carol Beasley waited. Carol also gave Victoria a journal, but this one was blank. It would be for Victoria to record her thoughts and memories, as well as prayers and answers to prayers. Years later Victoria could present it to her own daughter during her rite of passage. Grandma Beasley had an intimate conversation with Victoria, and talked about her side of the family and experiences. Victoria had her Bible, with her and a highlighter to mark verses.

PARTNERS *in the* PASSAGE

I LOVE MY CHILDREN and my grandchildren, and to think that something that I tell them might make a difference

in their lives and the decisions they make is a great responsibility. I knew I would have to choose my words carefully, with
love and kindness. I remember telling her how proud I was of
her because of her love for God and obedience to her parents.
I told her I thought she had chosen her friends wisely, and I
knew whatever she decided to do, she would be a success.

—*Carol Beasley*

Victoria's Mom on Character

Grandma closed with a prayer with Victoria and then sent
Victoria to the chapel, where her mother waited with a special gift. This was the final stop on the "trail" for Victoria.
Sheila talked with her daughter about Proverbs 31: "A wife of
noble character who can find? She is worth far more than
rubies. Her husband has full confidence in her and lacks nothing of value. She brings him good, not harm, all the days of her
life" (vv. 10–12 NIV). This passage is so rich in meaning for a
young lady entering adulthood. It symbolically describes everything a young woman should aspire to, keyed on noble character. And what would "noble character" consist of? Faith,
hope, love, integrity, purity, and all the other things talked
about during the rite of passage.

To provide a lifelong symbol of the Proverbs 31 wife, we
had purchased a ruby necklace that Sheila would give her.
The custom-made necklace had one ruby in the middle to
symbolize Victoria and several smaller rubies around the circle
to symbolize the accountability group of ladies who were
praying for her and encouraging her. After speaking with Victoria about being a woman of good character, Sheila presented

Victoria with that necklace. She prayed for Victoria and brought her back to the atrium, where we were all waiting.

PARTNERS *in the* PASSAGE

MY MOM IS THE PROVERBS 31 woman. Yes, she spoke to me about what it means to be one on this day, but she has shown me through her actions for years. I always knew she had been praying for me and supporting me as a mom, but on this day it was like she was saying that she was praying for me and supporting me as a woman and a friend.

—*Victoria McBride*

A Special Luncheon

While Sheila participated in the rite, at our home some dear women in our family prepared a luncheon. They set a beautiful table, anticipating our arrival. As I had done with my boys, when we got to the table, we had a time of conversation. Victoria soaked in the fellowship and love of these older women. After we finished the meal, we cleared the table, and I stood up. One by one, going around the room, I affirmed each woman who had participated in the ceremony and thanked her for being such a support and prayer warrior for Sheila and me. I asked them to stand and look Victoria in the eye and to make that same commitment to her—to be a prayer warrior, an encourager, and someone from whom she could seek godly counsel.

Then I turned to my older daughter and said, "There is a time in every woman's life when a young girl sits down but a

woman stands up. I want to encourage you and tell you that
whatever problem you might be having, you need to seek the
wise counsel of these women. God intends for us to seek godly
counsel, and when we are praying through decisions, we cannot
isolate ourselves.

"These women have committed to being that godly counsel and prayer warriors for you. When you reach the tough
times of your life, these are the people you need to call on.
These are the people who are committed to praying for you
and loving you."

I then asked her to stand up and look the women who
were standing in the eye and commit to calling on them for
godly counsel and wisdom in the days ahead. She then sat
back down.

"You Are the Crown on My Head"

"I know at this point you aren't married, but if you would
allow me to take the liberty as the key man that God has in
your life right now, I would like to tell you, from your father,
that you are a crown to my head. You have honored me and
your mother in your walk with the Lord, the way I see you
doing your personal Bible study, the way I see you praying
and seeking God for wisdom. You have been a crown to my
head, and you've honored me and your mother."

I then pulled out a full crown and placed it on her head.
"I want you to take this crown as a symbol of the godly character that your mother and I have observed in you, and I want
you to put it in your room on your dresser or some other significant place as a constant reminder to you to pray for the man
who you will one day marry, that you would be a crown on his
head by your observance and living your life for the Lord.
Then one day, when you do marry, that you would move it to

your bedroom to be a constant reminder to you and to him of your desire to be a crown to his head in the way you honor him and love the Lord."

PARTNERS *in the* PASSAGE

MY DAD SAID, "You have been a crown to my head. I hope that one day you can pass this on to your husband." This just speaks volumes, hoping that one day I will be as great a wife as all these women who spoke to me that day. They each gave me a little nugget on being a godly woman, but also a godly wife and mother too.   —*Victoria McBride*

I then asked Victoria to sit in a rocking chair that had belonged to my great-great-grandmother. All the women gathered around that chair in the middle of the room; then each prayed in turn for Victoria. Then I laid my hands on her head and prayed a prayer of spiritual blessing from Psalm 34 and Psalm 1. It was a great time of blessing, and we took a lot of photos to commemorate the day.

Three down, with one more to look forward to. It would soon be time for my youngest child, Sarah, to have her own rite of passage.

Six

SARAH'S TURN

A fter three previous rites of passage, now it was Sarah's turn. Sarah would go on a "journey" around the church in similar fashion to her sister. During that brief journey she would *separate* from her parents, *transition* through the teaching of wise women, and then be *incorporated* into the family and the larger community, there to be confirmed as an adult and sent into the world with our blessing.

She had just turned eighteen when her time came. Once at the church, Sarah and I walked to the area near the Prayer Tower. I explained I wanted to pray with her and told her this would be a special day, a time for her to pass from being a young girl to becoming a woman.

Harriet's Special Gifts

Her first station was again in the Prayer Tower, where she spoke with her great-aunt Harriett. As she had with Victoria, Harriett now spoke to Sarah on the phone about integrity, telling her no one can be a person of integrity without the Word of God. Only by following the teachings of Jesus would Sarah find and value the truth (John 8:31–32).

In addition to a special Bible that Sarah would use along the "trail," her great-aunt presented two very personal gifts. The first was a songbook Harriet had received from her own great-aunt, Rivers Washburn, which Great-aunt Rivers had purchased at the Ridgecrest (North Carolina) Christian Conference Center. The second was a CD that included one of the gospel songs from that old songbook, "The Solid Rock." Great-aunt Harriet included a personal note of encouragement with one of the gifts.

PARTNERS *in the* PASSAGE

I USED JEREMIAH 29:11, "'For I know the plans I have for you,' declares the Lord, 'plans to prosper you and not to harm you, plans to give you hope and a future" (NIV). I gave her a songbook that was bought at Ridgecrest by her great-aunt in 1930 with the song "The Solid Rock." ("My Hope is found in nothing less than Jesus' blood and righteousness.") I closed with a CD of "My Hope is in the Lord" and "The Solid Rock."
—*Harriett Golden*

THAT WAS PERSONAL, because everyone in my family knows how I am, how I relate, how I give off my emotions, and that has always been through writing. That meant a lot to me, the personal note, and I still use personal notes today, writing about my emotions.   —*Sarah McBride*

Again, having a mentor who knows your child is important. Sure, this was her great-aunt, but she also knew how Sarah related to the world, and the handwritten note was the perfect touch.

Jackie on Purity

Sarah then went to the bridal suite. There she met Jackie Harmon, the wife of her former youth pastor, Keith (who had participated in the ceremonies with Buddy and Tommy). Jackie talked to Sarah about purity and what it means to be part of the bride of Christ, living a life worthy of belonging to Christ.

PARTNERS *in the* PASSAGE

THAT WAS SPECIAL TO ME, because Jackie doesn't live here anymore. She mentored me for a long time, and I got really close to her family: her husband, who was our youth minister; and her son, because I baby-sat him a lot. That meant a lot to me that she traveled to be there. She was one of the number-one people I wanted there. She had constantly poured into me, and she was one of those people I really looked up to.   —*Sarah McBride*

WE TALKED ABOUT what purity means and what it looks like. It is not just sexual purity, but it is purity in every area of life; in what you watch, in what you listen to, the kind of places that you go, the people that you hang out with. We very much control that area of our lives. —*Jackie Harmon*

Jackie spoke on Sarah's future path and God's good plan, and how they related to her being pure before Him. She quoted Isaiah 55:8–9, where God says, "'For My thoughts are not your thoughts, nor are your ways My ways. For as the heavens are higher than the earth, so are My ways higher than your ways and My thoughts than your thoughts."

PARTNERS *in the* PASSAGE

SOMETIMES WE MAY THINK that we are supposed to be on a certain path or that we are supposed to do a certain thing, but God's ways are much bigger than ours, and through life we are all going to make mistakes. That doesn't mean that we have to live by those mistakes; our mistakes do not define us, but who we are in Christ defines us.

—*Jackie Harmon*

That was a great lesson for a young lady. At that stage of life so many young people are uncertain exactly what they want to do or what they believe God wants them to do.

Jackie then gave Sarah a purity ring, which symbolized not just the life of purity she was to live but also symbolized her status as a bride of Christ, secure in God's love and grace. It was a strong lead-in to the next person and topic Sarah would encounter.

Love Ribbons from Reneé

Jackie prayed with Sarah and escorted her to the choir room, Sarah's next station, where her aunt Reneé Warren waited. Reneé talked to her about what it meant to be a woman of love. It was a message different from what a lot of people expect when the subject is love. She did not use the standard passage, 1 Corinthians 13.

"Everyone uses Corinthians when they talk about love—the 'love is patient, love is kind' kind of things," Reneé later explained. "Instead, I told her that love is tough—that you need to love even when it is hard, that you need to love no matter what, as God loves us. Whether bad circumstances or good circumstances, you need to love."

This was an especially powerful message for Sarah, because she knew that at that time her aunt was going through a rough patch in her own marriage. Reneé quoted *The Greatest Thing in the World*, by Henry Drummond (see below), and focused on 1 John 4:7–11, which concludes, "This is love: not that we loved God, but that he loved us and sent his Son as an atoning sacrifice for our sins. Dear friends, since God so loved us, we also ought to love one another" (NIV).

PARTNERS *in the* PASSAGE

I USED A QUOTE FROM *The Greatest Thing in the World*: "Where love is, God is. He that dwelleth in love dwelleth in God. God is Love. Therefore love. Without distinction, without calculation, without procrastination, love. Lavish it upon the poor, where it is very easy, especially upon the rich, who often need it most, most of all upon your equals, where it is very difficult."

— *Reneé Warren*

Reneé embodied the toughness that is sometimes required by love. Even during the hard times in her own marriage, Reneé did not give in to anger or bitterness. Instead, she chose to love. She had brought some pieces of ribbon she had used on her wedding day to tie up her Bible. She talked about what the love of Christ meant to her and the love of her life, her husband, and how those ribbons had been used in her wedding ceremony. She gave Sarah a gift of two of those ribbons that symbolized the bond of marriage, even during tough times. The ribbons were tender but strong, soft but resilient. Those ribbons were the perfect gift to symbolize the type of love that Reneé emphasized for Sarah.

A Family Ring and a Coin from Grandma McKinney

After Reneé prayed with Sarah, she sent her to meet Grandma McKinney, who would talk to her about family. Her grandmother knew both Victoria and Sarah well, and she was sure to tailor her talk to each of them to fit their personalities, which is yet another good endorsement of choosing your speakers well. She encouraged Sarah to use the gifts God had given her and assured her that her personality type was chosen by God for His purposes.

PARTNERS *in the* PASSAGE

WITH SARAH I DID it a little differently from what I did with Victoria. Sarah is more like me; we are very independent, and we are very strong-headed. I wanted Sarah to understand that even though we may not like what our parents are saying, we still love and obey them. We can have our differences, but we still love them.   —*Norma Jean McKinney*

Then her grandma gave her two special, personal items, a ring and a rare coin. "My grandmother talked to me about our family legacy," says Sarah. She recalled the personal nature of the two gifts from Grandma. "She gave me one of her rings, which had a lot of sentimental value for her. She gave me a coin, too. It was a rare coin, something very personal to her."

Karen's Faith—and Sarah's

In the chapel Sarah met Karen Jorgensen, one of our church secretaries, who also assists with the youth ministry. She has known Sarah since she was a little girl.

Karen is a cancer survivor, so she had a lot of things to say about perseverance and faith. The two had already spent time together in Karen's discipleship group. Because of that relationship, I think Sarah's time with Karen was the most special. Sarah calls Karen's role during the discipleship group one of mentoring.

"She always took on a mother's role for me, mentoring me, talking about her life experiences," Sarah said later. "When I was younger, I had made the typical accepting-Christ decision, but I think I was just too young to understand it. She taught me how to love God, how to live as a Christian, and that it was more than just rules."

Sarah talked with Karen "for a long time during the rite." They reviewed the things Karen "had taught me and the experiences we had gone through."

PARTNERS *in the* PASSAGE

I LET HER KNOW what God did for me during my time with breast cancer. I had surgery and six months of chemo. At times I would be so afraid I wouldn't want to go to sleep. That's the time that I really feel that God did a work in my life. I got to know Him in a more intimate way than I had ever known Him before.

I shared with Sarah a special verse on trusting God, Isaiah 26:3 (NIV). "You will keep in perfect peace those whose minds are steadfast, because they trust in you." I told her no matter what might happen in her life, "God is there with you, waiting for you to talk with Him and to have a daily walk with Him. Don't stray from Him but always hold His hand. Let Him be the one who gives you that peace and that joy in life and that sense of purpose every day."   —*Karen Jorgensen*

At the end of their time together, Karen gave Sarah a booklet on a journey through faith. The deep relationship between Sarah and Karen shows again the power of adults to speak into the lives of children

Sherie on Hope

Sarah then spent time with her Aunt Sherie Baker, who had spoken to Victoria about faith. This time she talked with her younger niece about hope. Again, because of a long-standing relationship, Sherie knew exactly how to customize her talk for Sarah.

"Sarah was a cheerleader, so I brought along a picture of her in her cheerleading outfit," Aunt Sherie says. "As we looked at the picture, I reminded her that cheerleading requires lots of spirit and the know-how to express it. As believers in Christ, our spirit (Holy Spirit) should be evidenced in all that we do, no matter who is around. I shared with her that there should never be a doubt as to who we are in Christ and to always let her spirit show."

A Necklace and Crown for Sarah

As with her sister, Victoria, Sarah's last station was in the chapel with her mom, who talked about her precious value as a woman. Sheila gave Sarah a ruby necklace, as she had done with Victoria.

Afterward, Sarah and all the participants returned to our house for a meal. I went through a similar ritual of personally thanking each woman for investing in Sarah's life in the past. I told Sarah that these women would now become a resource for her to turn to for godly counsel. As with Victoria, I told her how Scripture says that a good wife is a crown on her husband's head and how, though she wasn't yet married, as a father she had been a crown on my head as a daughter.

I then presented her with her crown, and then all the women gathered around Sarah and individually prayed for her. The event ended with my prayer of spiritual blessing over her life. Then we took pictures, and that was the end of the event.

About the Rings, Swords, and Crowns

For all our children, Sheila and I paid for the key gifts presented during the rite of passage: the purity ring for each, the necklace and the crown for each daughter, and the sword for each son. My wife and I bought all the gifts. Though most of the participants also presented personal (and fairly inexpensive) gifts, the major gifts were from Sheila and me. I look forward to Victoria's and Sarah's weddings, for when the marriage ceremony is about to begin, I will say a few words and take the purity ring. Then I will walk her down the aisle; afterward I will give back the purity ring as a keepsake—and one day, perhaps, she will pass it on to her own daughter during her rite of passage. My sons have kept their purity rings at their homes as a reminder to remain pure in marriage.

You may wonder about the cost of buying such gifts for the rite of passage. A simple silver ring for the boys costs about fifty to seventy-five dollars with the engraved Scripture verse. As single men, they wore their rings regularly, except while playing sports. Once they were married, they replaced them with their wedding bands. The ruby necklace for the girls cost more, of course. We chose to make each necklace with real rubies (though small-sized ones). If you choose to present a necklace, I recommend buying real (rather than synthetic) rubies, to demonstrate the value of a woman "of noble character [being] worth far more than rubies" (see Proverbs 31:20 NIV). You can choose either kind of ruby for your customized necklace, but this is an item where you want to shoot for the best, if possible.

With the luncheon and the final prayer of blessing upon Sarah complete, I had intentionally and purposefully commissioned each of my children into adulthood. In the process my wife and I had communicated important biblical truths while also reinforcing a community of believers whom they could rely on for guidance, even as they themselves entered adulthood and raised their own children.

Others have performed similar ceremonies with their children, and in the next chapter they suggest some ways you might do so yourself. The final chapter describes how you might bestow a father's blessing on your adult child. The ideas in the remaining chapters will show how you too can meet your child's deep-down desires.

Seven

PLANNING
A RITE OF PASSAGE

What's the best way to design a rite of passage for children? Maybe you figured it out from chapters 3 through 6 . . . that's a trick question. There is no single, best way to conduct a rite of passage. As parents, you should adapt and modify the rite based on your individual children. But I can't overemphasize the power of these rites to affect your children's lives.

Now some of you might be saying, "Well, my son and I don't have a bad relationship . . . but we are not particularly close either. Plus there's no group of men or women that I could readily call on."

Finding the Influencers
in Your Child's Life

Yet, as the pastor declared when I was saved (see chapter 1): "It doesn't matter whether you are the sweeper in the company or the CEO of the company—there is somebody who looks up to you. There is somebody you have influence over, somebody who is modeling their life after you."

There also are adults who your son or daughter looks up to. Whether you're aware of them or not, they're there. You only need to make sure they are godly influencers.

Begin to pray about how you can arrange this event for your son or daughter. At the same time, try to identify who some of those influencers might be. They can be relatives; they can be high school football coaches or former soccer coaches who continue to encourage your child. They can be youth pastors. They can be men or women who are teaching in Sunday school, public or private school, or perhaps they are band directors. Somewhere along the line you have met or know about these people who influence your children.

You may not have a great relationship with those influencers. Maybe they have a better relationship with your child than you do, but you want to begin to form a bond with these men or women in order to put this rite together. Keep in mind that your event doesn't have to be identical to mine. Feel free to customize it for your children. It may be only you and two other men. In that case, have them speak on two topics apiece. Try to include a member of the family who knows your child well, maybe a grandparent or your girl or boy's favorite aunt or uncle.

It might be that your group has to be smaller. It might be that you have to do a little more work to identify who these men or women are.

Another obstacle might be your present relationship with your child. Perhaps you're not that close. You may need to take your child on a date, where you can relax together and talk about their week or month. You can make the time to attend school activities with her, whether a game, play, music concert, or something else. Whatever you do, don't just spring it on him or her from out of nowhere. If your child senses the rite is forced or phony, it might do more harm than good. It might be that you have to do a year or maybe more of preparation, of spending time and working through a process with your son or daughter to prepare him or her for this moment.

As we've seen with my children, the adults I chose all had an established relationship with the child, some more extensive than others. All knew my children well, well enough to customize their program to suit the personality of the child. And all had a strong relationship with God. As you consider your participants, look for those two elements. Your participants and potential mentors should have a solid relationship with your child and a solid walk with God. Influence can run in two directions, and by your choice of men or women you want to be sure that they'll influence your child in the *right* direction.

Remembering the Reasons for the Rite

Whatever you do, try to at least do *something* for your child. *This lets your child know that you love him or her* and that as a godly parent you are giving them blessings. *The rite also tells your child that you are recognizing a level of maturity* in his or her life. It is worth investing your energy in planning and preparation for this time. Those are just two of the reasons to have a rite of passage.

In the Marines we had a form of training we called OJT: on-the-job training. That meant you didn't go to a formal class to learn something. You were just given that job, and you were expected to learn along the way and get the job done. When it comes to raising children, I think a lot of people have an OJT mentality: parenting is on-the-job training. A lot of our children are going through life suffering from OJT, experiencing a lot of headaches and hiccups that they would not otherwise experience if we as parents were setting them up for success.

Remember too another key reason for this event. *With this rite of passage you and your child can take a lot of ground from the enemy.* You are preparing your son, who is becoming a man, for the many challenges Satan seeks to throw against him. You are seeking to help your daughter get ready for the spiritual challenges that will continue through her adult life. Therefore be wise and take care in identifying this group of men or women who are going to be the spiritual counsel or spiritual advisors for your child.

How Other Parents Have Planned Their Children's Rite of Passage

As I've noted throughout, each child is different, so you don't need to do it my way. Just remember the three components —*separation, transition,* and *incorporation*—and conclude with a blessing. But to give you more ideas and examples of what could work with your children, let's look at what other parents have done to customize the rite of passage for their children, including Coach Jimmy Fields, who participated in my sons' rites of passage.

Being Intentional

My friend John Spencer, like me, came to the realization that he needed to be deliberate in how he moved his children from youth into adulthood. He saw so many parents, even in the church, who had no sense of purpose in raising their children.

"The biggest thing about doing rites of passage is the intentionality," John says. "Part of the process for us was to make sure that we were the main input in their lives, that we weren't leaving it to someone else or expecting someone else to do that. I asked myself, *How do I make sure my kids aren't just following somebody else because they think it is cool?* How do I let them know there is a better sense of purpose that God has for them?"

That's an important insight. All too often I see parents involve themselves in every aspect of their kids' sports programs or after-school events and even their school schedules. Yet when it comes to raising them in the faith, to showing them how and why they should be living a certain way, they think that's the church's job—the pastor's, the youth leader's, or someone else's. It's not. Scripture tells us it's *our* job to raise our children in the faith. God says, "These commandments that I give you today are to be on your hearts. Impress them on your children. Talk about them when you sit at home and when you walk along the road, when you lie down and when you get up" (Deuteronomy 6:6–9 NIV). Remembering God's Word and teaching it to our children should be part of our everyday activities. It should be as much a part of us as walking down the road, getting dressed in the morning, walking out the front door.

The rite of passage, then, becomes part of a pattern. It's a special event, and the child should feel special as a result, but it shouldn't come out of the blue, either. It's part of a pattern of sharing your faith, of being intentional in dealing with your children.

I think we all need to be careful here, too. A rite of passage, no matter how special or how well planned, might leave the child bewildered—"What was that all about?"—or even cynical if you haven't been intentional in the child's life up to that point. Remember how Robert Lewis, in *Raising a Modern-Day Knight*, talked about a *process* for moving a child into adulthood.

Jackie Harmon, who participated in my daughters' rites, offers this warning: "I do think [the rite of passage] is a great thing for parents to do, but if you as a parent haven't been the spiritual leader and kept an eye on your children, if you have not raised them in a way that doing a rite of passage would resonate, then it would almost be counterproductive."

Marking Multiple Milestones

But if you've been intentional with your children and want to do something for them, you might even consider marking more than one passage in life. The authors of *Spiritual Milestones* recommend several key occasions, such as purity vows at age thirteen; a rite of passage at age fifteen or sixteen; and near the child's high school graduation around age eighteen.

John Spencer looked at the Jewish bar mitzvah that marked the passage of boys to men at age thirteen, and decided that was when he would begin his children's rite of passage. "I didn't want just one event; I wanted to have a few steps along the way. I wanted events where my children could say, 'Here is where my parents challenged me to place a stake in the ground and take the next step.'"

Spencer did this with his four oldest children—Kaitlyn, now nineteen; Kelsey, sixteen; Jud, fifteen; and Juliana, thirteen —and plans to do this with his youngest, Melody, who is age ten at this writing. He looked around the world we lived in and realized that he could not just allow his children to drift into adulthood with no specific guidance from their parents.

"We began the process with my oldest, Kaitlyn. When she turned sixteen, we took her out to eat, and I bought a nice ring. Her mom and I sat her down and talked to her about purity, and talked about what a lady should be expecting."

John's wife, Heather, also contributed with the girls, taking them out on mother-daughter dates and, as John describes, "teaching mother-daughter things to form in them some maternal and ladylike values."

Kaitlyn's Formal Rite of Passage

When Kaitlyn graduated from high school, they conducted another rite to celebrate that, something John plans to repeat with each of his daughters. She graduated on a Friday night, and Saturday morning she was introduced to her rite of passage. John included the pastor's wife, Kaitlyn's aunts, some other strategically chosen whom Kaitlyn has looked up to in her life, and her mom. "I gave them specific things to talk about, whether it was integrity or hard work or purity or whatever. We created a path around the church, and Kaitlyn would go to a room and speak to a lady and spend probably twenty minutes or so with that woman. Each gave her something as a token of their subject. We gave her a journal that she began that day so she could write those things down. So she kind of completed a circuit with six women that morning."

As I did with my children's rites, Kaitlyn's ceremony ended with a special meal. Before the luncheon, John and Heather went in and gave her a necklace that featured a little gold crown with rubies in it.

"I want you to always remember that your worth is far above rubies and far above jewels," John told her, "and that you will one day be a crown for some man's head. But, between now and then, you are still under my protection," John said, with his wife at his side, "and first and foremost we want you to be a woman who loves God, who is called for His purpose."

Jud's First Milestone

With his son, Jud, John started earlier, when Jud was approaching age thirteen. He asked Jud to read *A Call to Die: A 40-Day Journey of Fasting from the World and Feasting on*

God by David Nasser; John read the book at the same time. (Because of work and school schedules, they paced the forty days over a few weeks, taking weekends off.) That book, John said, forces the reader to consider what it means to confess faith in Christ and to live that life daily, dying to self, as Christ calls us to do. It's a message that runs counter to everything our culture tells us.

Studying that book led to John's next plan—and Jud's first milestone. Together they undertook an overnight hike in the nearby forest. In a way it was the separation phase of the rite of passage, although in this case Jud didn't physically separate from his family, since his dad was with him. It was, however, a separation from his everyday world. (Journeys into the forest or some other wild or semi-wild area are good for this.)

Jud had just turned thirteen when they hiked twelve miles on the Pine Mountain Trail of Franklin D. Roosevelt State Park in southern Georgia. "I wanted to do something that was going to stretch him physically," says John. "I'm not sure if it pushed him as much physically as it did me.

"We spent two days walking the trail, freezing that night together, but as we sat around the campfire, just he and I, I took out a nice knife I had brought. It was bone handled, almost like a Bowie knife. I presented that to him and talked about how he was going to have to start learning how to handle the Word of God as his offensive weapon. I told him that while he wasn't quite ready for a sword yet, he needed to start learning and apprenticing to do that. That knife was symbolic of that, taking him to that next step."

That experience in the woods was the transition phase, where Jud learned a bit about himself as he hiked an arduous trail and also as his father taught him. The presentation of the knife and returning home was incorporation back into the larger world and family.

Preparing Mighty Men

Another friend, John Hemken, also chose to use multiple opportunities to commemorate a life-passage with his boys: Ben, twenty-one at this writing; Andrew, now nineteen; Luke, now seventeen; and Daniel, now fifteen.

Of his methodical preparation and the milestones leading up to the rite of passage, Hemken says, "We as parents prepare our kids for everything else in life, to a fault. We prepare them for going to kindergarten, we prepare them for the ACT test, we prepare them for college, but what do we do to prepare them in character and manhood? We leave it up to the church; we leave it up to the youth pastor; we leave it up to anyone else. I said, 'Nope, that is my responsibility, not the church's.'

"I am a firm believer in incremental steps leading to a long-term relationship, which leads to long-term change."

Years ago John and I first discussed Robert Lewis' *Raising a Modern-Day Knight*. We were really struck by the metaphor. And we were also moved by the idea of mighty men of valor that you find in Scripture. Soon John would call the time spent with his then-young boys "our mighty men time."

"I was always stuck on that notion of raising a modern-day knight," John recalls, "and I was wondering, *Why am I leaving it to chance, my young men growing into maturity?* The feminization of our society works against growing boys to be men. I asked what was I doing to proactively and purposefully grow my sons into men. This is just like how they brought a boy into knighthood. You didn't grow knights by just being around, by osmosis. It was a very purposeful and very deliberate process.

"I can't think of a more important thing for me as a business owner. I grow leaders in my business, but none of that is more important than growing leaders in my children, growing godly men in my sons."

John chose age sixteen as the time to have a rite of passage ceremony with each son. He took them to a family cabin they have on a plot of land north of Green Bay, Wisconsin. It's set on forty acres of beautiful timber on a river in a restored log cabin. It's a *Swiss Family Robinson* kind of place: remote, wild, but with the comforts of home. Hemken brought the mentors up early and briefed each on what his role was to be. They would have a time of fellowship, too. (I was honored to be one of those men.)

Hemken made sure the men had an already-established relationship with his boys and that he also knew them well. To do this, he had started preparing the men and his sons long before it came time for the ceremony, bringing them together in a "mighty men group." It had been an eight-week study using Promise Keepers material, beginning when the boys were in the sixth grade.

The Mighty Men of Scripture

The concept of "mighty men" tells a lot about what John tries to do. We know of the mighty men of the Bible through the account found in 2 Samuel 22–23. These were the men who journeyed with David into the wilderness and were devoted to him, even taking great risks to serve and protect him as they ran for their lives from King Saul and his assassins. David was the anointed and future king, yet Saul treated him as the enemy. Still, David's mighty men stood with him. From this concept John built his "army."

"Who Will I Hang Out With?"

He began when each boy was in the sixth grade. "That is a transition point for young men," John says.

"A boy at that age might be asking, 'Who am I going to hang out with?' So rather than leave it to chance, I said, 'Let's pick some dads and sons that we want to hang around with, and let's do life with them for a little bit.' Then, by definition, that became for my boys who they hung around with. We created their peer group in the sixth grade.

"I would find other dads and sons, and we would go through that together, because that helped us dads prepare how to do this as much as the sons. I guess we kind of grew our own mentors in the sixth grade groups that ended up continuing on in my sons' lives. They were the invitees at the sixteen-year-old's rite of passage."

When it came time for the ceremony, the boy's mother, Kathleen, brought the son up to the Wisconsin cabin. She used the opportunity of the trip to bless her son, and upon arriving she walked him down to the cabin. There she would have a memorable challenge, customized for each boy. Once at the cabin, the boy would meet his maternal grandfather, Merle. He always took on the teaching of family and passed on the importance of family. After Merle finished, he would send the boy down a small path, where he'd meet the next man. They'd talk about purity, trust, honesty, or the fruits of the spirit.

The advantage of having several sons is that the older boys got to participate in the ceremony for their younger brothers. John especially remembers the most recent rite of passage, for their son Luke.

"His two older brothers were able to take part, and that was incredibly meaningful. We called it joining the brotherhood of the mighty men. As the dad, I had the privilege of going last, and [I asked his older brothers] to share what they learned. I was able to affirm him, both as his dad and as a brother in Christ."

For each of his sons, John had all the participants return to the cabin once the stations are completed. They'd circle up and, with each man in the company of everybody else, John affirmed the son. He then affirmed every man around the circle.

"I did borrow one of Jim's ideas, where I present a sword to my son. Each one has been different, but it's a medieval sword of some kind with the date, the boy's name, and all the men that were there inscribed on it. All my boys have them hanging in their rooms as a reminder, along with the various gifts that they got from the different men on their support team."

Some Fine-Tuning

One thing John did was fine-tune the rite to each individual boy's temperament. As Proverbs 22:6 (NIV) says, "Train up a child in the way he should go, and when he is old he will not depart from it." Train a child according to his natural bent, his inclinations, and he will also be on the right road.

John knew Luke's love language—the way he feels most loved—is to hear words of affirmation. "Being the number three son, he feels like number three sometimes, and he really needs to be made to feel special. With Andrew, he is not the most outgoing of our kids, so the theme was 'be bold in the Lord.'"

A Daughter's Rite of Passage

For many fathers, our first inclination is to plan a rite of passage for our sons, because we feel comfortable with other males. But don't miss out on the blessing you will receive as a father when you take the time to call out the woman in your daughter.

Dee Kelley, who participated in Victoria's rite of passage, works with her husband to prepare parents for the idea of purposefully moving their children through the various life stages, even if it doesn't mean doing the exact thing we did. For daughters and sons alike, parents have a great opportunity to prepare and release their children into adulthood, according to Dee.

"We speak to a small group of parents each year, between ten and twenty families in a class. There is so little out there for . . . parents who [want] to be totally involved in their kids. We pray for them in this direction, we'll lead them in this direction, but they have to want to be active in doing something for their kids through all stages of their childhood and into their adulthood. This rite of passage encourages parents to let them go in a healthy manner and gives them a sense of knowing it is okay to let them go. They are going to be okay when they go out into the world because they are going to have this group of women or men to help them stay accountable."

Sherie Baker, who participated in both Victoria and Sarah's rites of passage, looks forward to someday doing the same thing for her little baby daughter, whom her husband and recently adopted.

"The Lord laid it on my husband's heart for us to adopt, and we did. He provided a family that chose us because He knew from the beginning that [Emma] was going to be our baby. She has been a blessing in our lives. I want to share a rite of passage with my daughter too. Victoria and Sarah will probably be my picks as speakers for her."

What could be more beautiful and meaningful than that? My two daughters, whose lives were blessed over the years by Sherie's faithfulness and Sherie's mentoring, could return the blessing and continue the tradition in a few years when young Emma comes of age.

How to Make Your Daughter Feel Loved

Many fathers who I know did not have a formal rite of passage for their daughters, yet they sensed the need to have a transition to mark their girls becoming women. The father knew his daughter soon would leave home, and he wanted to deepen their relationship before she left.

Such fathers arranged a special getting-away-from-everything for the two of them. For some fathers and daughters, the two participated in a major construction or medical project—a mission outreach with some time alone. The fathers told me how working hand-in-hand with their daughters while serving Christ brought about a lifelong memory and marked their child's passage into adulthood. One dad took his daughter to Disney World. They not only built their relationship, but through their activities and time together they created a lifelong memory—and, indirectly, the father marked a time of transition to womanhood for his daughter.

Such events do not substitute for a rite of passage, of course. But they do remind your daughter of her value to the family, of your love for her, and of the fact that she is becoming a woman. If you are not able to have a rite of passage, for whatever reason, do consider planning for such a time to elevate your daughter and let her know, through the gift of a special time together, that you love and value her.

Special Ideas for Special Kids

The best way to honor your child, though, is through a formal rite of passage. That doesn't mean you have to do your rite as I did mine. As we noted earlier, children are different. There are no cookie-cutter kids; all are unique. There are different ways to approach the rite of passage, depending on the parent or the child. Some parents create a prayer box or a prayer jar when their child is young. They write down all the prayers they've prayed for their children over the years and put them in the box or jar. They then give this to the child when he or she comes of age.

Imagine what it would be like for a son, now grown up, to go back and read that his dad was praying for him when he was struggling in school back in the fifth grade. Imagine a daughter reading her mother's prayers for her as she went through that rebellious stage at age twelve. Nothing communicates a parent's love and devotion to their child like seeing that "prayer trail" that extends into the past. It would go a long way toward putting some of those hurt feelings and angry words into context.

If you think your child—or you—wants it to be low key, you don't have to invite five adults and set your son or daughter on a trail as part of the rite. Jimmy Fields, the football coach who participated in both Buddy and Tommy's ceremonies, chose to keep it simple when his son Jay turned sixteen. He and another man took Jay into the wilderness for trout fishing. The occasion wasn't as formal or elaborate as some others, but he intentionally chose that time to initiate Jay into manhood and to inculcate his specific calling as a man. The most important thing was that it was deliberate and purposeful—a time set apart to call a son to manhood.

Special Situations

We recognize that not every parent lives in an ideal world. Maybe they came to faith later in life or as an adult. Maybe they didn't grow up in a Christian home. Maybe they're new to the faith, new to the church, and haven't had the opportunity to have a lot of Christian men and women minister into their lives.

As Youth Pastor Keith Harmon, notes, "Some may say, 'My son, my daughter, they haven't had the privilege of having five or six men or five or six ladies who are part of their lives and who love them the way that this book talks about.' They don't live in what sounds like a perfect-world scenario.

"But you know, maybe there are two people. Maybe it is a dad or a mom, a Sunday school teacher, a scout leader, a cheerleading coach, an art teacher, a band director; maybe there is someone that mom or dad knows who has really meant a lot to their child and shares the same values that they do."

Other parents might be afraid to consider doing a rite of passage for their children because of their own pasts. How can they encourage their children to purity when they haven't lived it themselves? How can they encourage integrity when their lives have shown anything but? The parent may think, *My kid knows that I failed. My kids have* seen *me do it wrong.*

To this, Harmon offers the following suggestion: "Your kids probably know that already, so make that a part of the ceremony. Say, 'I know I have not been the best mom. I know I have not been the best dad, but I want to start today.' I think teenagers would love to start today. I have never seen, in fifteen years of youth ministry, a student who was unwilling to forgive, who was unwilling to try, who was unwilling to give their parents a chance."

What if you're a parent at a church, and one of your children's friends attends church or youth group with them but doesn't come from a Christian home? Maybe one parent is a believer and the other not, or maybe neither is. Shouldn't that child still have the opportunity to have some adults in his life to bless him, affirm him, and usher him into manhood?

Garrett Grubbs, a youth pastor, knows that situation very well. "I grew up in a home where Mom and Dad weren't really active in church, and so they didn't provide the accountability of sexual purity or any other accountability. It was provided through a relationship with my youth pastor and also a group of friends who were believers. If you grow up in an environment where you are involved in church and have a relationship with Christ, but you live in a secular home, there is a lot of stumbling around as to what culture communicates it means to be a man. Maybe it's even what your father is communicating. So you, as a child, are trying to understand what it means to be a man biblically, but it is difficult."

Pastor Grubbs recalls a boy whose mother comes to church but whose father attends rarely. The dad, a very successful businessman, has little spiritual interest. "You have the son coming to church but the father almost pulling him away."

Such a situation can be very sensitive. You must respect the rights and privacy of the parents, but you also feel a duty to help the young man or woman grow into Christian adulthood. What should you do? As an adult man who wants to support this boy in his journey to manhood, you can do something. The most effective approach would be to meet with both parents to present the purpose of the weekend, says Grubbs. You can also invite them to be involved with it, to be exposed to what is happening. "I would sit down with the parents to say, 'This is what the weekend looks like. Here are the different stages, and this is the end goal: to have this group of people, including you, placing a blessing on your child to pursue the Lord and live out Christ with his life.'"

This is, as I said, a sensitive situation, and you should seek godly counsel from your pastor and from others who know the family. Most important, approach the situation with prayer. The timing has to be right, and the approach has to be right. A rite of passage has the potential to be a great evangelistic outreach to the family, a great blessing, but it also has the potential to cause the parents to withdraw their child from the church or youth group and perhaps the only positive influence in the child's life. The answer? Pray and seek wisdom before considering such an action.

The beauty of doing a rite of passage is that it can be something that passes from generation to generation—a heritage and a blessing.

When You're a Participant

Participants in a rite of passage are men or women who have an influence on the life of a maturing child. With your involvement in your church and your neighborhood, it's possible you will be asked to participate in another child's rite of passage. If so, keep these guidelines in mind.

- You are part of a life-changing event. It is an honor to have been asked to be a part of a rite of passage. That you have been asked indicates you already have a level of influence on this child's life.
- Your words will have an impact, so seek God for wisdom. Prayerfully seek Scripture on the topic that you will speak on.
- There is a time of commitment at the end of the rite, when the father will ask you to be a part of the child's "board of directors," a counselor and mentor who can give advice and encouragement. Make sure you are comfortable with being available for that role (except those rare times when your schedule prevents it).

Don't let the importance of the occasion cause you to be fearful or hesitant that you will say or do the wrong thing. It is not so much what you say. Your presence on that special day speaks volumes to the child. You gave your time and in some cases perhaps made a long trip to be there. The boy or girl will appreciate your being there and welcome your words, even if they are not eloquent or always inspiring to you.

Eight

OUTCOMES

A rite of passage is an event. But it represents much more than that, and now that I've conducted the rite of passage for my four children, I realize there are certain things I want to remain with them for a long time. As you plan the rite of passage for your children and consider the partners you would invite and gifts or tokens they might give, consider these truths.

First, the gifts are Ebenezers or, as I called them, the memorial stones (see 1 Samuel 7:12; Joshua 4:6–8). The gifts your children receive from the adults during the rite should be things they hold on to, cherish, and remember. I have seen that with all four of my kids.

Memories for the Present

The girls still wear their ruby necklaces, and they keep the crowns in their rooms. While dating, Victoria told her boyfriend,

Mark, about the ruby necklace her mom gave her during the rite of passage. When he proposed to her, he chose to add rubies on each side of the diamond ring.

Those gifts will have an impact on your children. They are visual reminders of the commitments they make and the love shown by family and mentors. In our family, the boys keep their swords on the wall in each of their rooms as a reminder, and both wore their purity rings until they were married. The girls still wear theirs. Those memorial stones and especially the heirloom gifts they received from their grandparents are all things they still hold on to as a reminder of that particular day.

A Heritage for the Future

There is a second outcome awaiting the child who participates in a rite of passage. With a family member and your spouse participating, your children can understand and learn to appreciate their background even more. This will prepare them to value both the past and to desire to carry a heritage into the future. Our son Tommy, for example, said the rite gave him a deeper sense of pride in his family and its legacy. And, as he prepared to get married, he got to thinking about what legacy he was going to pass on to his children. So as the wedding planning continued, the idea of a special ceremony and ritual came to mind.

"Kelly's family goes to our church, and they hold a lot of the same values. We knew that at our wedding we wanted to be characterized as a praying couple," Tommy said.

He remembered seeing at some weddings the couple using a prayer bench. Perhaps you've seen them. They consist of a small, padded kneeler and a framework that holds a flat surface that can be used to hold a Bible or hymnal. Some are quite simple in design, others quite elaborate. Tommy thought what better way to symbolize his wish that he and Kelly be known as a praying couple than to make a prayer bench for him and his new bride.

Tommy visited a lumberyard and bought some rough-cut mahogany from South America and built the prayer bench. Now, he didn't have a lot of carpentry experience, but that didn't matter so much; this was a work of love. It took him months, but the time he spent working on it meant a lot. The night before the wedding, they brought the bench to the front of the church. At the end of the ceremony, they knelt at the bench, and I came up to the altar and prayed over them. Then Kelly's dad and I signed the bottom of the bench and each wrote a message so that fifteen generations down the road, the future McBrides would see a message of the family legacy. After the wedding, Tommy and Kelly moved the prayer bench to the foot of their bed. Now every night they come to that prayer bench and they pray as a couple before going to bed.

"Through my rite of passage I learned [to incorporate] the traditions of our family and the traditions of our faith . . . into our marriage," Tommy says. "I went from being a sixteen-year-old boy who was worried about football to a man who is raising a family and loving his wife, and living the legacy shown to me. With the rite of passage, it is really in your face that this is what it means to be a godly Christian Man."

A Third Outcome: Spiritual Counsel

A third outcome of a rite of passage is the spiritual counsel available to the child. Your child knows he or she can call one of the participants years later; your child will have an advisor who can listen and offer perspective. And from time to time, your then-adult children *will* seek counsel. From time to time I'll talk to the football coach or the youth pastor or one of the ladies, and they will say, "Guess who called me today?" One of my kids will have contacted them, asking them to pray about something or requesting their counsel on a particular situation. And that was one of your goals all along—to have a group of men or women your child could call on for prayer and counsel.

With so many influences and so many people speaking into their lives as adults, you will be grateful they are calling on praying, God-fearing people to help them make the hard decisions of life. And your children will be grateful for this ready band of counselors as well.

To me the ultimate outcome of the rite of passage is the helping your children tie into a group of spiritual advisors and mentors.

"A lot of those guys are still a big part of my life," says Tommy's older brother, Buddy, "and I know whenever I have a question I can call any of them and get good advice."

Knowing You Are Loved

The blessing that concludes the rite of passage brings a final long-term outcome to your children. For the kids to hear that their parents are proud of them is such a blessing. That is not just a one-day, one-moment thing you say. In the context of the event and how we lived before and after, both the rite and the blessing that concluded it helped Sheila and me continue to have our children's hearts. We are still very much involved in their lives, and they call on us for spiritual counsel to help them pray through the big decisions in their lives, keeping that connection.

Part of being successful as a parent is not that your children turn out perfect but that your children continue to strive to be who they are supposed to be in Christ, that they are continuing on the path to sanctification. Yes, maybe they fall, but they get back up, and their eyes and their hearts are still focused on the Lord. You, as the parents, can still have good communication with them and can be part of that journey with them. The blessing upon your child can have a lifelong impact in opening communication and letting them know you really love them.

Hearing a parent bless them, knowing that you are their advocate, gives your children confidence for the life ahead. They know that with this blessing a parent is going to cheer them on and help them as far as it is possible to accomplish their goals in life.

Don't underestimate the importance of cementing your relationship with your children as they enter adulthood. Don't take it for granted that just because you successfully raised them and sent them on their way, they will always have a good relationship with you. An unfortunate truth is that a lot of adult children do not get along with their parents. A recent study in the journal *Psychology and Aging* found that the "parent-child relationship is one of the longest lasting social ties human beings establish. This tie is often highly positive and supportive but it also commonly includes feelings of irritation, tension and ambivalence."[1] Psychiatrist Harry Bloomfield adds that almost 90 percent of children in adulthood do not get along with their parents.[2] Those are tragic findings.

That relationship might have been close as the children grew up and then left the nest, but over the years any number of things, from lifestyle choices to child-rearing styles or even politics and religion can cause a rift. But if you have raised them right and established a firm basis for their faith, rooted in your affirmation of them and in giving them a solid group of mentors to turn to, the chances for later conflict can be diminished.

And there may be a time when they will bless you in return, thanking you for your active demonstrations of love. That affirmation will give you confidence and comfort as well. Here are words from Victoria we still cherish.

"Being in your early twenties and being in college, you still think that you know everything," says Victoria. "Just seeing how my parents loved me enough to do that and to share those experiences with me and all these other people—it means more now. Being out on my own, I have more of a need to cling to those lessons and those Scriptures they gave me.

"The more I look back on it now, I see the influence of it. It was a point where my parents sat down and said, 'We trust you, we know who you are, and we believe you are learning who you are.' I just think it is so important for any child to receive that from their parents."

Epilogue

IT'S NEVER
TOO LATE

When asked how he could be a better dad, I once heard a father say, "Well, my kids are all grown, so I really don't have anything to say here." He thought his job was done and he no longer had a responsibility to love and affirm his children.

Why would he say that? Why would he want to? As long as your children are still your children, you are still a father, even if you are ninety and they are seventy. You are still a father; you are still a mother. So to me, the definition of parental success is to have your children walking in the faith and still in a good relationship with their parents, and you being involved in their lives.

Perhaps, though, some parents might feel guilty. They did not have the greatest relationship with their children, and now the children are grown and out of the house. Perhaps a parent never had a chance or never took the opportunity to tell a child he loved him. Here's my advice: *It's never too late as a dad to affirm your child—to tell him you love him unconditionally, to let her know you love her always.* If you can't meet, call (or Skype) your son or daughter. If that's not possible, write a personal letter expressing your love.

I think there are some adults walking around today who never had the experience of a parent affirming them and telling them they were loved. I have sat in many small discussion groups with grown children, and two statements I have heard over and over again are, "I never heard my dad say he loved me," or "I never knew if I had my dad's approval."

Receiving the Blessing as an Adult

I always knew my dad loved me, but he'd never said it to me explicitly. We did not have a bad relationship, but we also did not have the type where my dad opened up to me. My special moment, a moment I consider a personal rite of passage, came when I knew for sure that I not only had my dad's approval but I had his blessing. And it wasn't all that long ago —I was a grown man.

I had long since left the carnival business, but sometimes as a family vacation Shelia, the kids, and I would help my dad for a week at a particular carnival spot. It was fun for me to be back doing what I knew, a way of reliving my childhood. It was also fun for my family, being on the inside, so to speak, seeing how a carnival runs. Besides, what could be more fun than spending your entire vacation at the carnival?

One week we met my dad at a carnival in Manassas, Virginia. There a ring, a most unusual ring, would affirm his love for me.

That ring traced back to an encounter with one of Dad's brothers, who, like all the men I can remember on my dad's side, were involved in the Freemasons. Masonry is a fraternal order whose origins go back in obscurity to the early stone-masons of medieval Europe. It is particularly strong in England and Scotland, where the McBrides are from, and it was prominent in the early years of our country. (George Washington is perhaps the most famous of our nation's early Masons.) As soon as I came of age to be qualified, I became a Mason.

A Ring of Value

My uncle Woody, who owned a carnival business and was a key mentor in my life, was also in the Masons. For the longest time, he wore this very nice, 32nd degree Masonic ring. It featured a double eagle with an old mine-cut diamond right in the middle of it. He had told me and my dad, who were both the next generations working in the carnival business, that whichever one of us became a 32nd degree Mason first, that would be the one he would give that ring to. I became a 32nd degree Freemason first, and as my uncle lay on his death bed, he gave me that ring.

But when I became a Christian, I really felt convicted about being in the Masons. You'll hear conflicting things about the Masons and Christianity. Some are true, some are not, and it's not my purpose here to hash them out. In short, I felt convicted, not about the aspects of whether Freemasonry had something occult or something else involved in it, but more from the standpoint that the organization was segregated. There were black Masons and there were white Masons, and they didn't mix. How could I love my African-American brother in Christ and be a part of something that he couldn't be fully a part of? Suffice it to say that upon being saved, I became uncomfortable about my membership in the Freemasons. I had long since become inactive, but still, my name would have been on the roll, and I still had this 32nd degree Mason ring.

So I talked it over with my wife, I prayed about it, and I contacted the Masons. I told them I wanted to be taken off the books and be taken out of their register. I no longer wanted to be a part of an organization like that. They thought I was crazy. They contacted some of my family members, and some of them called me and asked me if I had lost my mind. Why, they asked, would I want to get out of this organization? I explained to them what I believed and how I was convicted about it.

Still, I requested to be dropped from the Masonic roles, and so I thought I was out of the Masons. But a year later again I received my dues card, saying they wanted me to pay my dues. I called them, and I asked, "Why am I receiving this? Last year I told you I wanted to be out of the Masons." They then explained that one of my relatives had come in and paid my dues last year. They were convinced I was just going through a phase and would soon "get over it." I told them, "Well, I haven't gotten over it, and I'm not going to get over it, and I want to be out of the Masons."

A Ring Renounced

I had a good idea who had paid my dues, but I really didn't care. I just went ahead and moved on and made it very clear I no longer wanted to be a Mason. So I was out. At that point my great-uncle's daughter, my dad's first cousin, contacted me and said, "If you are out of the Masons, you're probably not going to wear my dad's ring anymore." I said, "That's right." She said she wanted the ring back for the family. She even offered to buy it, telling me I could keep the diamond, sell it, and give the money to my church. She just really wanted that ring.

I said I had to pray about it, but I added, "I know this: Your dad gave me this ring in one piece, and I'll either keep it in one piece or I'll give it to you in one piece, but I'm not going to separate the diamond and the ring." After praying about it, I felt the Lord was leading me to just put it in a box and give it to her and ask for nothing—just send it to her. Remember, this was an old mine-cut diamond, and the ring had been appraised at $2,500.

So I sent it off to her and asked for nothing. I didn't hear any more about it.

My Dad's Words

Now, months later, my family and I were at this carnival to help Dad. We worked all day and night. One night, after the carnival had closed, we were raking up all the trash. It was around midnight, and there was no one else around—just me and Dad. My dad called me over to his side as we were both holding our rakes, and he put his arm around me. Then he said, "You don't even know that I know what you did with that ring. But I heard about what you did. I am really proud of what you did and the way you did it—asking for nothing.

"When you told me you loved God, that didn't mean nothing to me," he added. At this point I thought, *Oh, my goodness, where's this going?*

Then he said, "But when I saw you living for God, that meant everything to me. That ring was a ring from your uncle, but I have this ring that belonged to your uncle that was made from gold melted down from a lot of different rings. It has seven diamonds in it. I don't know the dollar amount, but it's worth far more than what that other ring was worth. I want you to have this ring as a symbol of connection to that uncle but also as a symbol of your father recognizing the fact that you're living and loving God with your life. I love you, and I'm proud of you."

He gave me that ring that night. It was a powerful moment I'll always remember. It was the first time I ever remembered my dad saying he was proud of me. Here I was, an adult with a family of my own, and this was the first time my dad had affirmed me. And even more powerful was the reason he affirmed me—for standing on principle and standing for my faith. My dad was not much of a believer at the time, and this was a great witness to him. Today he tries to attend church regularly, and his carnival schedule is less demanding—he only stocks and operates food stands. Significantly a midweek Bible study is on his schedule, and he runs concessions for Upward Sports, a sports ministry at his church.

To me that midnight moment with Dad years ago says a couple of different things: It says that faithfulness and obedience are followed by blessing. It says that you can't out-give God. I gave away one thing unconditionally, and He gave me in return something far more valuable. I gave away a ring from a person who had been a key mentor in my life, and God gave me back a ring from that mentor through the hands of my father—with a blessing.

Maybe you can or have had a moment of blessing for you, a time with your parent.

Helping Your Child to Become an Adult

In *Raising a Modern-Day Knight*, Robert Lewis recounts the story of Sam Rayburn, the speaker of the House of Representatives. Representative Rayburn was one of the most influential legislators to ever walk the halls of Congress. The Rayburn Congressional Office Building in Washington is named after him. As Lewis begins the story, Rayburn was a young man growing up in Texas:

> One particular day in 1900, surrounded by the windswept Texas prairie, Sam's dad had hitched the buggy

and driven his 18-year-old son to town. The boy was going off to college and would be leaving the farm that his father, a poor man, had tilled his whole life. Standing together on the railway platform, father and son awaited the approach of the train. Sam's "suitcase"—actually, a bundle of clothes tied with a rope—lay at his feet. No words were spoken.

Then, when the train arrived and Sam prepared to board, his father reached out and placed a fistful of dollars into his hand. Twenty-five dollars. According to Robert Caro [Rayburn's biographer], "Sam never forgot that; he talked about that $25 for the rest of his life."

"Only God knows how he saved it," Sam would say. "He never had any extra money. We earned just enough to live. It broke me up, him handing [me] that $25."

With tears in his eyes, Sam turned to board the train. Again his father reached out and grasped his hands. The four words he spoke would echo forever in the boy's memory. He said, simply, "Sam, be a man!"[1]

"Be a man!" What more powerful thing could a father say to his son?

"Be a woman of God!" What more powerful thing to say to a daughter?

That simple conversation between my dad and me one summer in my late thirties is that same experience to me. I will always look back on it as Sam Rayburn looked back on his dad sending him off into the world.

To any father, to any man, if you are alive and your children are still breathing, it's never too late for you to have a moment, a rite of passage, or a time of blessing between you and your child, a time when you affirm him, look her in the eye, and acknowledge your love and respect for them.

It's never too late.

SAMPLE OUTLINES
FOR PLANNING
A RITE OF PASSAGE

Outline of the Boy's Rite of Passage

The father prays with his son to begin the rite of passage. Then he takes his son to the first of the stations, where the first participant is waiting. Here are the suggested topics for each of the stations:

- Station #1:   Integrity
- Station #2:   Purity
- Station #3:   Faith
- Station #4:   Hope
- Station #5:   Love
- Station #6:   Family

After the final participant completes his time with the son, everyone returns to the beginning of the trail. The father then invites the participants in the rite of passage to join him and his son for lunch (or dinner).

Before and during the meal, the adults and the father enjoy regular conversation. The son will probably want to just listen in, but if he's comfortable, invite him to join in the conversation. After the meal, begin the rest of the ceremony:

- Affirmation of participants by the father
- Challenge and calling out of the son
- Presentation of the father's gift—the sword
- Prayer by members of the group
- The father's prayer of blessing

Outline of the Girl's Rite of Passage

The father prays with daughter to begin the passage. Then he takes his daughter to the first of the stations, where the first participant is waiting. Here are the suggested topics for each of the stations:

- Station #1:   Integrity
- Station #2:   Purity
- Station #3:   Faith
- Station #4:   Hope
- Station #5:   Love
- Station #6:   Family

After the final participant completes her time with the daughter, everyone returns to the beginning of the "trail." The father then invites the participants in the rite of passage to join him and his daughter for lunch (or dinner).

Before and during the meal, the adults, including the mother and father, enjoy regular conversation. The daughter may want to just listen in, but if she's comfortable, invite her to join in the conversation. After the meal, begin the rest of the ceremony:

- Affirmation of participants by the father
- Challenge and calling out of the daughter
- Presentation of the father's gift—the crown
- Prayer by members of the group
- The father's prayer of blessing

NOTES

Introduction: Why a "Rite"?

1. Robert Lewis, *Raising a Modern-Day Knight: A Father's Role in Guiding His Son to Authentic Manhood*, rev. ed. (Carol Stream, Ill.: Tyndale, 2007), 10.

2. As cited in Cathy Lynn Grossman, "Young Adults Aren't Sticking with Church," *USA Today*, 7 August 2007 at http://www.usatoday.com/printedition/life/20070807/d_churchdropout07.art.htm.

3. The Barna Group, "Most Twentysomethings Put Christianity on the Shelf Following Spiritually Active Teen Years," 11 September 2006, http://www.barna.org/barna-update/article/16-teensnext-gen/147.

4. As quoted in Grossman, "Young Adults Aren't Sticking with Church," *USA Today*.

5. Brian D. Molitor, *Boy's Passage, Man's Journey* (Lynnwood, Wash.: Emerald Books, 2004), 17–18.

6. "The Gang Threat," FBI press release, 6 February 2009, http:\\www.fbi.gov/news/stories/2009/february/ngta_020609/.

Chapter 1: Rites and Blessings

1. Jerry Moritz in e-mail correspondence to Tom Neven, 24 June 2010. Moritz has taught at the International Chrisitan Ministries Seminary/African Theological Seminary for eleven years in Kitale, Kenya, and has interacted with the Maasai people.

2. John Wesley, *Wesley's Explanatory Notes*, 1 John 2, 1754–54; http:\\www.Biblestudytools.com/commentaries.

3. Brian D. Molitor, *Boy's Passage, Man's Journey* (Lynnwood, Wash.: Emerald Books, 2004), 120.

Chapter 2: Developing the Idea

1. Jim and Janet Weidmann and J. Otis and Gail Ledbetter, *Spiritual Milestones* (Colorado Springs: Focus on the Family, 2001), 12.

2. Ron Dunn, *Don't Just Sit There . . . Have Faith* (Amersham-on-the-Hill, Bucks, U.K.: Scripture Press Foundation, 1994), 38.

3. C. S. Lewis, *The Four Loves* (New York: Houghton Mifflin Harcourt, 1991), 3–4.

4. Warren Wierbe, *Be Quoted* (Grand Rapids: Baker, 2000), 84.

Chapter 4: Tommy's Turn

1. Mike Rich, *Radio*, Columbia Pictures, 2003.

Chapter 5: Victoria's Rite

1. Brian and Kathleen Molitor, *Girl's Passage, Father's Duty* (Lynnwood, Wash.: Emerald Books, 2007), 21.

Chapter 8: Outcomes

1. "Study of Relationships between Adult Children and Parents," *Medical News Today*, 6 May 2009; at http://www.medicalnewstoday.com/articles/149047.php.

2. Carol Kuykendall, *Give Them Wings* (Wheaton, Ill.: Tyndale, 1994); cited at http://www.troubledwith.com/Relationships/A000001203.cfm.

Epilogue: It's Never Too Late

1. Robert Lewis, *Raising a Modern-Day Knight*, rev. ed. (Carol Stream, Ill.: Tyndale, 2007), 9.

ACKNOWLEDGMENTS

A mong the many individuals who made this book and my ministry possible, I begin with Sheila, my wife and best friend. The woman who knows me best loves me most, which I'll never take for granted. You frame the best years of my life (twenty-eight and counting). Our kids are blessed to be your kids, and I love you with all that I am, your forever Honey Bunny.

To Victoria and Mark, Buddy and Mallory, Tommy and Kelly, and Sarah, thanks for giving me joy immeasurable. Thank you for so many rich memories and, as our family continues to grow, for all that lies ahead.

I am also grateful to Michael Catt, senior pastor, mentor, and friend. In my years at your side, I have grown to be a better father, husband, and executive pastor by learning from your example. Again and again God has used, and uses, you to shape my family and me into the image of Jesus Christ, for which I'm eternally grateful.

My thanks to Mandy McGuire, who has served as my administrative assistant these last four years. You have supported me by always making sure I was where I needed to be when I needed to be there. You take every opportunity to make things excellent, and I am grateful to serve the Lord alongside you.

James G. McBride Sr. is my father and lifelong hero. Thanks for giving me a ring and that moment in time that I can now use to help other men bless their children. Norma McKinney is my mother and my lifelong number-one cheerleader. So much of the man I am points to the woman you are.

How I appreciate my wordsmith, Tom Neven. Without you this book would still be in random files and rough paragraphs. Thanks for helping turn the ideas on my heart into words on a page.

I am especially grateful to Greg Thornton, Randall Payleitner, Carolyn Shaw, Jim Vincent, and all the right people at Moody Publishers. Who knew that a team in Chicago could accomplish so much for this man in Albany, Georgia? Thank you for believing in me.

Finally, to Bill Reeves, my agent, brother in Christ, and friend: thanks for encouraging me start to finish.

RITEOFPASSAGEBOOK.COM

Visit RiteofPassageBook.com …

a site dedicated to inspire and assist you in conducting meaningful rite of passage experiences for the young men and women in
your life. You'll see videos of Jim McBride explaining why he
wrote the book and describing the ceremonies he created for his
sons and daughters. You will find links to sources for obtaining
special keepsakes so the experience lives on. And you will be
able to share your story and read stories of others who are putting to use the principles taught in the book.